ANNE WILLAN'S
LOOK&COOK

Chicken Classics

ANNE WILLAN'S
LOOK&COOK

Chicken Classics

DORLING KINDERSLEY
LONDON • NEW YORK • STUTTGART

A DORLING KINDERSLEY BOOK

Created and Produced by
CARROLL & BROWN LTD
5 Lonsdale Road
London NW6 6RA

Editorial Director Jeni Wright
Copy Editor Norma MacMillan
Art Editor Mary Staples
Designers Lyndel Donaldson
Wendy Rogers
Lucy de Rosa
Lisa Webb

First published in Great Britain in 1992
by Dorling Kindersley Limited
9 Henrietta Street, London WC2E 8PS

A CIP catalogue record for this book is available
from the British Library
ISBN 0-86318-862-1

Reproduced by Colourscan, Singapore
Printed and bound in Italy by A. Mondadori, Verona

CONTENTS

CHICKEN

THE LOOK & COOK APPROACH

Welcome to **Chicken Classics** and the *Look & Cook* series. These volumes are designed to be the simplest, most informative cookbooks you'll ever own. They are the closest I can come to sharing my techniques for cooking my own favourite recipes without actually being with you in the kitchen looking over your shoulder.

Equipment and ingredients often determine whether or not you can cook a particular dish, so *Look & Cook* illustrates everything you need at the beginning of each recipe. You'll see at a glance how long a recipe takes to cook, how many servings it makes, what the finished dish looks like, and how much preparation can be done ahead. When you start to cook, you'll find the preparation and cooking are organised into easy-to-follow steps. Each stage is colour-coded and everything is shown in photographs with brief text to go with each step. You will never be in doubt about what it is you are doing, why you are doing it, or how it should look.

🍽 SERVES 4-6   🍲 WORK TIME 25-35 MINUTES   🍵 COOKING TIME 20-30 MINUTES

I've also included helpful hints and ideas under 'Anne Says'. These may list an alternative ingredient or piece of equipment, or sometimes the reason for using a certain method is explained, or there is advice on mastering a particular technique. Similarly, if there is a crucial stage in a recipe when things can go wrong, I've included some warnings called 'Take Care'.

Many of the photographs are annotated to pinpoint why certain pieces of equipment work best, or how the food should look at that stage of cooking. Because presentation is so important, a picture of the finished dish and serving suggestions are at the end of each recipe.

Thanks to all this information, you can't go wrong. I'll be with you every step of the way. So please, come with me into the kitchen to look, cook and create some outstanding **Chicken Classics**.

Anne Willan

WHY CHICKEN?

Chicken is so versatile that mastering a range of chicken recipes is one of the most useful things for a cook. Sold in so many forms, chicken can be dressed up to grace the most elegant dinner table or simply cooked to provide the basis of innumerable everyday meals. Chicken can be prepared in many different ways, delicious on its own, cooked in a sauce, or combined with all sorts of vegetables and even with shellfish. Traditional accompaniments add even more character, differing from country to country and often depending on the cooking method employed.

RECIPE CHOICE

Practically every country in the world has a favourite chicken dish, and my selection of recipes attempts to marry traditional cooking styles and ingredients with the wide variety of chicken cuts available. Here's an overview of the chicken classics old and new that you will find in this book. To make your choice easy, they are grouped by type – whole birds, pieces, breasts and cooked meat.

WHOLE BIRDS

A whole bird, simply roasted, is widely served throughout Europe and America, and the French method of roasting chicken in a fairly high heat guarantees the most successful result. My four recipes use this method. *Chicken Château du Feÿ*: a bird is stuffed with herbs and roasted with butter. *Roast Chicken with Lemon*: a whole lemon gives additional character. *Roast Chicken with Lemon and Herb Butter*: bird is 'self-basted' with flavoured butter under the skin. *Roast Chicken with Garlic*: roasted garlic cloves add flavour and thicken the sauce.

A full-size chicken can also be poached. *Yorkshire Chicken with Stuffed Prunes*: a chicken is poached with breadcrumb-stuffed prunes and a rich velouté cream sauce. *Chicken in Parsley Sauce*: velouté sauce is flavoured with plenty of parsley and lemon.

If flattened to cook evenly, a whole chicken can be grilled. *Grilled Chicken with Garlic Herb Butter*: split and flattened, the chicken is spread with garlic herb butter and grilled. Small-sized chickens or poussins are also delicious grilled. *Grilled Poussins with Mushroom Sauce*: mustard adds bite to a flavoursome, rich mushroom sauce.

These small chickens are delicious pot roasted, too. *Chicken en Cocotte with Lemon and Parmesan*: small chickens are cooked in a covered pot with lemon and served with a zesty sauce. *Chicken with Thyme*: sprigs of fresh thyme add flavour to chicken baked in a pot. *Chicken en Cocotte with Juniper Berries and Wild Mushrooms*: earthy juniper berries and wild mushrooms are natural partners for chicken. *Stuffed Poussins with Grapes*: small chickens with couscous stuffing are served with red or green grapes and a sauce made with port. *Stuffed Poussins with Chilli Sauce*: fiery harissa in tomato sauce adds spice to these couscous-stuffed little birds.

CHICKEN PIECES

A whole chicken, cut up, provides four, six or eight breast and leg pieces, or pieces can be bought pre-packaged. They can be cooked in a number of ways. Sautés involve browning the chicken pieces then cooking them in their own juices with the addition

of various liquids, other flavourings and occasionally, other ingredients. *Sauté of Chicken with Paprika*: a Hungarian accent is given with paprika, red peppers and soured cream. *Szechuan Pepper Chicken*: sautéed chicken goes oriental with spicy Chinese pepper. *Sauté of Chicken with Beer*: stout and a jigger of gin inspire this recipe. *Sauté of Chicken with Mussels*: the saltiness of mussels provides the flavour, green beans add colour. *Chicken with Clams*: clams are delicious when combined with chicken.

Two dishes that depend on frying. *Southern Fried Chicken with Pan Gravy*: the unbeatable American classic. *Bacon-Fried Chicken*: bacon fat adds piquancy to this fried chicken.

From North Africa come two casseroles that require diffused heat. *Moroccan Chicken Baked with Spices:* cinnamon, ginger and saffron highlight the apricots and honey in this classic dish. *Moroccan Chicken with Aubergine:* chicken with an offbeat combination of aubergine and lemon, coriander and cumin making it highly seasoned.

Chicken pieces can also stand up to more prolonged cooking. *American Brunswick Stew:* a rich stew with broad beans and sweetcorn thickened with potato. *Chicken with Kidney Beans and Garlic Sausage:* this hearty stew is a meal in itself. *Chicken Stew Basquaise:* tomatoes and roasted peppers produce the classic Basquaise flavour.

Three of my dishes improve by being prepared ahead. *Chicken in Red Wine:* classic 'Coq au Vin'. *Chicken in White Wine:* medium-dry white wine is the base for this light sauce with onions and mushrooms. *Chicken in Beaujolais:* this light, fruity red wine is delicious with chicken.

Chicken pieces are ideal for eating with the fingers. *Devilled Drumsticks with Warm Potato Salad:* a piquant spice mixture for barbecued chicken legs, great for outdoors. *Devilled Chicken Wings:* perfect food for a crowd.

And less expensive cuts can make unusual fare. *Grilled Chicken Thighs in Yogurt:* yogurt tenderises the chicken and creates a spicy sauce. *Grilled Chicken Thighs with Yogurt and Honey:* tangy and sweet, this sauce grills well.

CHICKEN BREASTS

Tender all-white-meat chicken breasts are the most expensive form of chicken to buy, but boning them yourself can make them more economical. *Chicken in a Paper Case with Julienne Vegetables:* these chicken breasts are great for a small dinner party. *Chicken in a Paper Case with Peppers:* sweet peppers accompany chicken breasts baked in easy-to-make paper cases.

Two easy stir-fry dishes use chicken meat cut into fine slices. *Oriental Stir-Fried Chicken:* a quick and tasty stir-fry. *Sweet and Sour Stir-Fried Chicken:* pineapple adds Hawaiian tang to this delicious stir-fry.

Chicken breast meat is ideal for kebabs, marinated cubes threaded on a skewer and grilled. *Indonesian Chicken Kebabs:* a delectable snack of spicy chicken served with a peanut sauce. *Vietnamese Chicken Kebabs:* ginger and lemon grass give a special flavour to these kebabs.

Poached chicken breast meat with contrasting filling on a pool of sauce is great for special occasions. *Pinwheel Chicken with Herbs and Goat's Cheese:* pretty pinwheel rolls are just right for an elegant dinner. *Pinwheel Chicken Italienne:* Parma ham and fontina cheese add Italian panache to pinwheel chicken breasts.

Finely minced breast meat is versatile for shaping and whisking into mixtures. *Chicken Pojarski:* a Russian recipe with a crunchy coating. *Cocktail Pojarski:* great, do-ahead snacks for a cocktail party. *Cold Chicken and Ham Pie:* a grand savoury pie perfect for a picnic. *Hot Chicken and Ham Pie:* zesty horseradish cream sauce accompanies this hot meat pie. *Chicken Mousse with Madeira Butter Sauce:* fluffy chicken mousse served with a luxurious butter sauce. *Cold Chicken Mousse with Tomato and Mint Coulis:* ideal for a festive summer lunch.

COOKED CHICKEN MEAT

Chicken is a favourite for salads both hot and cold. Start with home-cooked roast chicken or buy it ready cooked. *Chicken with Curry Dressing and Saffron Rice:* a spicy variation on chicken salad. *Chicken with Tarragon Dressing and Rice:* the sweet aroma of tarragon is a classic partner for chicken. *Tex-Mex Chicken Salad:* tomatoes, sweetcorn, and peppers form a sunburst of colour. *Cobb Salad:* a Californian favourite with blue cheese, bacon and avocado.

Use cooked chicken, too, as a filling for hot pies. *Chicken Pot Pies with Herb Crust:* scones top cooked chicken and diced vegetables. *Large Chicken Pot Pie:* a warming meal for a cold winter's day.

EQUIPMENT

Cooking chicken requires very little specialised equipment and usually standard tools can be substituted.

A chef's knife or poultry shears is needed to cut up a chicken and a boning knife is useful when boning breasts or removing a tendon. All knives should be sharpened regularly and stored carefully to prevent dulling.

A trussing needle and string may be necessary to tie a whole bird into shape. Metal skewers can be used for trussing, as well as for holding chicken kebabs and flattened chicken pieces down for grilling. Bamboo skewers are attractive for serving kebabs, but they must be soaked in water to keep them from scorching during cooking. A meat mincer or food processor is important for minced chicken dishes; the meat tends to jam in a blender.

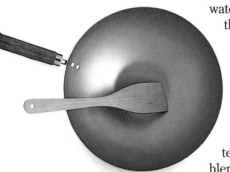

INGREDIENTS

Chicken goes with an astonishingly wide variety of ingredients.

Butter is essential for adding a crisp golden skin to roast chicken but in many other recipes olive oil, and flavoured nut oils, are taking its place.

A full range of fresh herbs – basil, tarragon, rosemary, oregano, thyme, chives – make a natural marriage with chicken, not to mention the often neglected common parsley. The neutral flavour of chicken blends equally well with spices such as nutmeg, cinnamon, curry powder, allspice and the zesty impact of chilli powder. Almost all vegetables complement chicken, from roots such as carrot and onion to greens such as spinach, plus tomatoes, peppers and the entire edible mushroom family. Shellfish combined with chicken adds salty flavour, a handy seasoning for the mild meat.

As for wine, many of the most famous chicken classics rely on red wine, white wine, and fortified wines such as sherry and Marsala for their character.

Chicken is one of the most economical sources of high-quality protein and, cooked without its skin, is lower in calories than most other meats. Light meat contains less fat and less cholesterol than dark, and chicken breast meat can be used in any recipe calling for pieces.

My recipes, like all traditional French cooking, use butter and salt as standard ingredients. If you are concerned to cut calories and fats, you can substitute polyunsaturated margarine or mono- and polyunsaturated oils for butter, but the results will not be as successful. A teaspoon or two of oil, preferably in a heavy-based, non-stick frying pan, may work for the sauté dishes. I usually don't indicate amounts for salt in recipes, as this should be to taste only, and the herbs and spices I use should make the dishes flavoursome without too much salt.

TECHNIQUES

If you master just a few techniques for working with chicken, you will be able to tackle a wide variety of recipes. For instance, removing the tendon from a chicken breast prevents shrinkage and makes the meat tender for serving. Cutting out the wishbone makes a whole bird easy to carve, while trussing ensures even cooking and an attractive shape.

Chickens are often sold already cut up into pieces, but if you cut up a chicken yourself, the pieces will be meaty and of an even size, while the bones from trimming can be used for making chicken stock.

Carving a whole cooked bird, cutting neat slices of both white and dark meat, has long been an art. Boning a cooked bird, discarding the skin so only the meat is left, is yet another possibility, often needed for chicken salad.

As with the other volumes in this series, there are techniques for preparing ingredients other than chicken. You will find how to chop herbs; how to skin, seed and chop tomatoes; how to peel and chop garlic, chop shallots, and slice or chop onions; how to clean and quarter or slice mushrooms; how to prepare and slice an avocado; how to cut julienne vegetables; and how to roast, seed and slice peppers, as well as make a bouquet garni and vinaigrette dressing.

CHICKEN CHATEAU DU FEY

🍽 SERVES 4-6   🥄 WORK TIME 20-30 MINUTES   🍲 COOKING TIME 1-1¼ HOURS

EQUIPMENT

carving board

conical sieve

small knife

kitchen paper

chef's knife*

2-pronged fork

large metal spoon

wooden spoon

aluminium foil

2 metal skewers

roasting tin just large enough to hold chicken

Here is a staple of our dinners at home in Burgundy – a classic roast chicken without a stuffing but with herbs inside for flavour. Its simplicity will make it one of your favourites, too. The butter used in cooking the chicken goes into the gravy so the more butter you use, the richer the gravy will be! You can present the chicken whole, as shown here, to be carved at the table or, if it is easier, carve it in the kitchen. Roast potatoes – crisp on the outside and tender within – are the perfect accompaniment to the moist, juicy flesh of the chicken.

GETTING AHEAD
There's really no way to reheat a roast chicken satisfactorily. However, the bird can be kept warm at least 30 minutes by wrapping it loosely in foil as soon as it comes out of the oven.

metric	SHOPPING LIST	imperial
2 kg	roasting chicken	4-4½ lb
	salt and pepper	
2-3	large sprigs of fresh thyme	2-3
2-3	large sprigs of fresh rosemary	2-3
1	bay leaf	1
60-75 g	butter	2-2½ oz
500 ml	chicken stock	16 fl oz

INGREDIENTS

chicken

chicken stock

butter

fresh rosemary

bay leaf

fresh thyme

ORDER OF WORK

1 PREPARE THE CHICKEN

2 ROAST THE CHICKEN

3 MAKE THE GRAVY

*carving knife can also be used

1 PREPARE THE CHICKEN

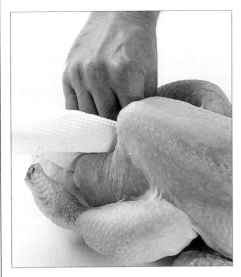

1 Heat the oven to 220°C (425°F, Gas 7). Wipe the inside of the chicken clean with kitchen paper.

2 Remove the wishbone from the chicken (see box, below left). Season the chicken inside and out with salt and pepper. Put the herbs inside the chicken.

ANNE SAYS
'Tarragon, oregano or any fresh aromatic herb can be used instead of the thyme or rosemary. Dried herbs are much less satisfactory.'

3 Set the bird breast up and push the legs back and down. Insert one skewer near the knee joint and push it through the bird and out through the other leg.

HOW TO REMOVE THE WISHBONE

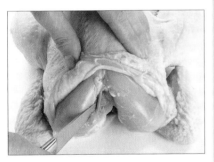

1 Fold back the neck skin of the chicken. With the point of a small knife, loosen the wishbone.

4 Turn the bird over so it is breast down. Pull the neck skin over the neck cavity and tuck the wing tips over it.

5 Push the second skewer through both sections of one wing and into the neck skin. Continue under the backbone of the bird to the other side. Push the skewer through the second wing in the same way, through both wing bones.

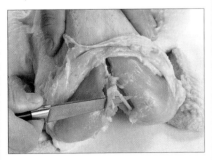

2 Remove the wishbone. Also remove any fat.

ANNE SAYS
'Without the wishbone, the breast meat is easy to carve into thin slices.'

6 Turn the chicken breast up again. It is now ready for cooking.

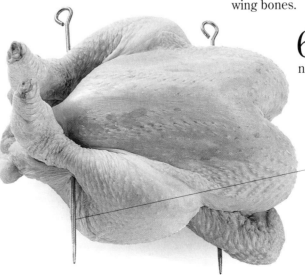

Skewers are shortcut way to hold chicken together instead of trussing

2 ROAST THE CHICKEN

1 Put the chicken in the roasting tin, breast up. Cut the butter into slices and arrange them on the chicken breast.

ANNE SAYS

'Adding butter to the chicken in this way enriches the meat and gives a characteristic golden colour to the skin. The quantity is up to you, but 60 g (2 oz) is a minimum.'

Sturdy metal roasting tin has low sides so oven heat can reach sides of bird

2 Roast the chicken in the heated oven for 1-1¼ hours, basting it with the juices in the tin every 10-15 minutes.

ANNE SAYS

'Frequent basting is the key to a juicy bird with well-browned, crisp skin.'

HOW TO CHECK IF A CHICKEN IS COOKED

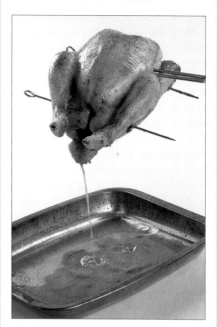

A chicken is thoroughly cooked when the juices from the cavity run clear. To check, lift the bird with a 2-pronged fork and tip it so you can see the colour of the juices that run out of the cavity into the roasting tin.

3 To keep the meat moist, turn the chicken on to its breast after it starts to brown. Return it breast up about 15 minutes before the end of cooking. Transfer the chicken to the carving board and cover with foil to keep warm while making the gravy.

3 MAKE THE GRAVY

Use conical sieve
when pouring gravy
to avoid spills

1 Add the stock to the roasting tin
and boil over high heat, stirring to
dissolve the juices. Continue boiling
until the gravy is thoroughly reduced
and concentrated.

ANNE SAYS
*'Boiling the gravy hard will emulsify the
butter and fat from roasting and thicken
the gravy slightly.'*

2 Taste for seasoning, then
strain the gravy carefully
through the conical sieve into a gravy
boat or serving bowl.

¶⊙¶ TO SERVE
Present the chicken whole, or carve it
(see box, page 14) in the kitchen and
serve on individual plates. Serve the
gravy separately.

Fresh herbs
such as
thyme,
rosemary
and bay leaf
give an
attractive
touch

Potatoes, roasted in
oil and butter, are an
ideal accompaniment

HOW TO CARVE A COOKED CHICKEN

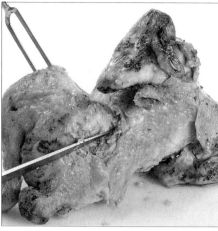

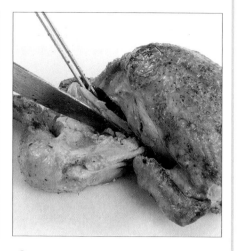

1 Remove the skewers. With a chef's knife, cut down between the leg and the body.

2 Turn the bird on its side and cut close to the backbone, leaving the 'oyster' meat attached to the thigh.

3 Turn the bird on its back again. Twist the leg sharply outwards to break the joint, then cut through it and pull the leg from the body. Repeat the procedure to remove the other leg.

Long-pronged fork keeps fingers clear of knife blade

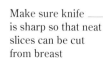

4 Halve the leg by cutting through the joint, using the line of white fat as a guide.

5 Cut horizontally above the wing joint, through to the breastbone, so you can carve a complete slice of breast meat.

6 Carve the breast in slices parallel to the rib cage. Cut off the wing. Carve the other side of the bird in the same way.

Make sure knife is sharp so that neat slices can be cut from breast

If necessary, slice meat from thigh so everyone has some white and dark meat

ROAST CHICKEN WITH LEMON

Replace the thyme, rosemary and bay leaf in Chicken Château du Feÿ with a lemon. If you can get an unsprayed, unwaxed lemon, so much the better.

1 Scrub the lemon, then roll it on the work surface to help release the juices. Prick it with a fork, place inside the chicken and roast the bird as directed.
2 When making the gravy, stir in a squeeze of lemon juice before straining it.
3 For serving, cut a fresh lemon into neat slices and use to decorate the chicken.

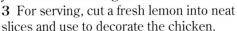

ROAST CHICKEN WITH LEMON AND HERB BUTTER

1 Prepare the chicken as directed in steps 1 and 2 of Chicken Château du Feÿ.
2 Finely grate the zest of 1 lemon. Strip the leaves from 2-3 stalks of fresh thyme and 2-3 sprigs of fresh rosemary. Cut the leaves into small pieces, then chop them finely. Beat the lemon zest and herbs into 60-75 g (2-2½ oz) butter.
3 In step 3 of the main recipe, lift the breast skin with your fingers and carefully ease it away from the meat; spread the flesh with the butter. Continue as directed in the main recipe, from the beginning of step 3.

ROAST CHICKEN WITH GARLIC

A garlic lover's dream: unpeeled cloves of garlic are roasted with the chicken, then crushed to thicken the sauce. Surprisingly, once the garlic has been cooked, it has a mellow, sweet taste.

1 Prepare and roast the chicken as directed in Chicken Château du Feÿ.
2 Separate the cloves from 1 head of garlic; do not peel them. Spread the garlic cloves in the roasting tin around the chicken when you first baste it, 10-15 minutes after it goes into the oven.
3 Make the gravy as directed, and when straining, crush the garlic against the side of the sieve to extract the pulp.
4 If you like, prepare a roasted garlic garnish: slice the top off 4-6 heads of garlic (1 per person), drizzle with a little olive oil and arrange in an oiled baking dish. Roast with the chicken, about 45 minutes. To eat, squeeze out the soft cloves of garlic.

DEVILLED DRUMSTICKS WITH WARM POTATO SALAD

🍽️ SERVES 4　🥣 WORK TIME 20-25 MINUTES　🍲 COOKING TIME 35-40 MINUTES

EQUIPMENT

chef's knife

small knife

bowls

pastry brush

metal spoon

whisk

saucepans

colander

chopping board

2-pronged fork

aluminium foil

ANNE SAYS
'*Poussins, one per person, can be used in place of the drumsticks. They will need only about 25 minutes cooking; serve them whole.*'

These spicy chicken drumsticks are archetypal barbecue fare, and are excellent cooked on a charcoal grill. Accompany with corn on the cob. For the potato salad, look for baby potatoes, or firm, waxy potatoes which will hold their shape when boiled.

metric	SHOPPING LIST	imperial
8	chicken drumsticks	8
	vegetable oil for grill rack	
	For the devil mixture	
125 g	butter	4 oz
30 ml	mango chutney	2 tbsp
30 ml	tomato purée or ketchup	2 tbsp
30 ml	Worcestershire sauce	2 tbsp
5 ml	ground nutmeg	1 tsp
2.5 ml	anchovy paste	½ tsp
	salt and pepper	
	cayenne pepper or Tabasco sauce	
	For the potato salad	
30 ml	red wine vinegar	2 tbsp
2.5 ml	Dijon mustard	½ tsp
90 ml	vegetable oil	3 fl oz
a few	sprigs of fresh parsley	a few
a few	fresh chives	a few
750 g	baby potatoes, or 4 large firm potatoes, peeled	1½ lb

INGREDIENTS

chicken drumsticks

butter

tomato purée

mango chutney

anchovy paste

Dijon mustard

cayenne pepper

fresh chives

vegetable oil

fresh parsley

potatoes

red wine vinegar

Worcestershire sauce

ground nutmeg

ORDER OF WORK

1 MAKE THE DEVIL MIXTURE

2 MAKE THE POTATO SALAD

3 PREPARE AND GRILL THE CHICKEN

1 MAKE THE DEVIL MIXTURE

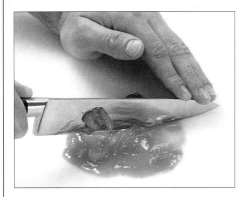

1 Melt the butter gently in a small saucepan. Chop any large pieces of fruit in the chutney.

2 Put the chutney in a small bowl and add the remaining devil mixture ingredients, with a pinch of cayenne pepper or dash of Tabasco sauce, and the melted butter. Mix together well, using the metal spoon. Taste for seasoning.

Spices mixed with liquids make tasty coating for chicken

2 MAKE THE POTATO SALAD

1 Make a vinaigrette dressing (see page 36) with the vinegar, mustard, oil and a pinch each of salt and pepper.

2 With the chef's knife, chop the parsley and chives finely.

3 If using large potatoes, cut each one into 2-3 pieces. Leave baby potatoes unpeeled. Put the potatoes in a medium saucepan of salted water and bring to the boil. Cover and simmer until tender when pierced with the point of the small knife, 15-20 minutes.

4 Drain the potatoes thoroughly in the colander, then cut into 9 mm (3/8 inch) thick slices. Transfer them to a large bowl.

Allow potatoes to cool a little before slicing

5 While the potatoes are still warm, add the chopped herbs and pour over the vinaigrette dressing; mix gently. Cover with foil and keep warm.

HOW TO CHOP HERBS

1 Strip the leaves or sprigs from the stalks. Pile the leaves or sprigs on a chopping board.

2 With a very sharp chef's knife, cut the leaves or sprigs into small pieces.

ANNE SAYS
'*When chopping a large quantity of herbs or sprigs of herbs such as parsley, hold them together in a bunch with your other hand while chopping.*'

3 Holding the tip of the blade against the board and rocking the handle of the knife up and down, chop until the herbs are coarse or fine, as you wish.

! TAKE CARE !
Do not chop delicate herbs such as basil and tarragon too finely because they bruise easily.

3 PREPARE AND GRILL THE CHICKEN

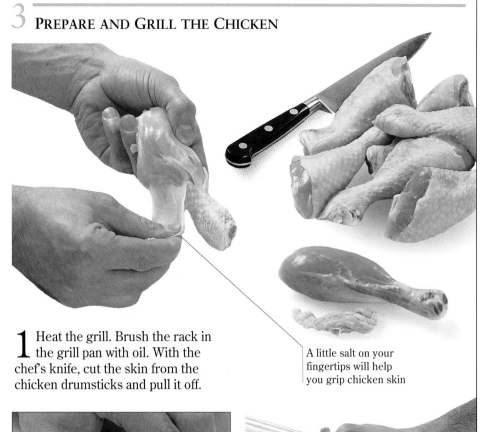

A little salt on your fingertips will help you grip chicken skin

1 Heat the grill. Brush the rack in the grill pan with oil. With the chef's knife, cut the skin from the chicken drumsticks and pull it off.

2 Slash the meat on each drumstick diagonally several times with the point of the knife.

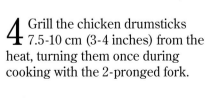

Brush on spicy coating

3 Brush some of the devil mixture over each drumstick, working the mixture well into the cuts in the meat. Arrange the drumsticks on the oiled grill rack.

4 Grill the chicken drumsticks 7.5-10 cm (3-4 inches) from the heat, turning them once during cooking with the 2-pronged fork.

DEVILLED CHICKEN WINGS

These tasty chicken nibbles are becoming popular as a pub snack and on wine bar menus.

1 Prepare the devil mixture as directed in the main recipe for drumsticks.
2 Substitute 12-14 chicken wings for the drumsticks. Cut off the wing tips and discard them, then coat the wings and cook as directed.
3 Omit the potato salad.

5 During cooking, baste the chicken drumsticks frequently with the remaining devil mixture and any pan juices. Cook until they are well browned and tender, about 10-12 minutes on each side.

¶❍¶ TO SERVE
Arrange the warm potato salad on individual plates, with the drumsticks alongside.

—**GETTING AHEAD**—
The drumsticks and salad can be prepared a day ahead and kept, covered, in the refrigerator. The drumsticks can be served either hot or cold. To reheat, wrap in foil and warm in a 180°C (350°F, Gas 4) oven about 10 minutes.

Devil coating on drumsticks can be as hot as you like

MOROCCAN CHICKEN BAKED WITH SPICES

¶◉⌐ SERVES 4 ⌣ WORK TIME 10-15 MINUTES 🍲 COOKING TIME 1½ HOURS

EQUIPMENT

tajine*

poultry shears saucepan

chef's knife

2-pronged fork

sieve

bowls

chopping board large metal spoon

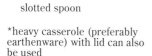

slotted spoon

*heavy casserole (preferably earthenware) with lid can also be used

ANNE SAYS
'*Small chickens are typical of Morocco, but you can easily substitute a larger one and cut it into 6 pieces. Larger chickens will require a slightly longer cooking time.*'

INGREDIENTS

onions

chicken

dried apricots fresh parsley

honey

tomatoes

saffron

olive oil

ground cinnamon ground ginger

This is a version of the classic Moroccan 'tajine', a mixture of chicken, fruit and spices baked under a conical earthenware lid. Any heavy casserole can be substituted, preferably made of earthenware to diffuse the heat. Instead of jointing the chicken yourself, you may prefer to buy it in 4 pieces.

GETTING AHEAD
The chicken can be baked up to 3 days ahead and refrigerated, or it can be frozen. Heat it in a 180°C (350°F, Gas 4) oven 20-30 minutes before serving.

metric	SHOPPING LIST	imperial
1.5 kg	chicken	3½ lb
	saffron	
45-60 ml	boiling water	3-4 tbsp
a few	sprigs of fresh parsley	a few
500 g	tomatoes	1 lb
6	onions	6
75 g	dried apricots	2½ oz
30 ml	honey	2 tbsp
10 ml	ground cinnamon	2 tsp
5 ml	ground ginger	1 tsp
	salt and pepper	
125 ml	olive oil	4 fl oz

ORDER OF WORK

1 JOINT THE CHICKEN

2 PREPARE OTHER INGREDIENTS

3 COOK THE CHICKEN

1 JOINT THE CHICKEN

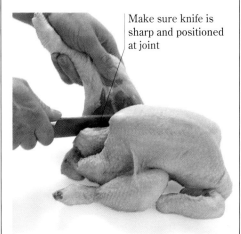

Make sure knife is sharp and positioned at joint

1 Using the chef's knife, cut down between the leg joint and body on one side. Twist the bone sharply outwards to break the joint, then cut through it and pull the leg from the body. Repeat this procedure for the other leg.

2 Slit the chicken closely along both sides of the breastbone to loosen the meat, then split the breastbone with the poultry shears.

3 Turn the bird over on to its breast and cut the rib bones and backbone from the breast in one piece, leaving the wing joints attached to the breast. The 2 breasts of the bird are now divided.

2 PREPARE OTHER INGREDIENTS

1 Put a large pinch of saffron into a small bowl. Spoon over the boiling water. Set aside to soak.

2 Chop the parsley. Peel, seed and chop the tomatoes.

Chop tomatoes coarsely with sharp knife

ANNE SAYS
'There is no need to peel tomatoes with thin tender skin, but do remove the seeds and surrounding juice because they would make the dish watery.'

HOW TO SLICE AN ONION

1 Peel the onion and trim the top. Cut the onion in half lengthwise, from top to root.

ANNE SAYS
'Leaving the root on helps hold the onion together during slicing.'

2 Put one half, cut side down, on the chopping board. Holding the onion firmly, cut it crosswise into slices, starting where the top has been trimmed and guiding the knife with your bent fingers. Discard the root when you reach it. Repeat with the other half of the onion.

Guide knife with your
bent fingers

3 Thinly slice 4 of the onions (see box, page 21). Finely chop the remaining 2 onions.

Hold onion firmly
while chopping

4 Cut the dried apricots into chunks using the chef's knife.

ANNE SAYS
'You can also use kitchen scissors to cut up the apricots.'

3 COOK THE CHICKEN

Spread mixture in
even layer over
tomatoes

1 Heat the oven to 180°C (350°F, Gas 4). Put the chicken in the tajine. Cover with the sliced onions, then with the chopped tomatoes.

2 Mix the chopped onions, saffron and its liquid, dried apricots, honey, cinnamon, ginger, chopped parsley, salt and pepper together in a bowl. Add the olive oil. Spoon the mixture over the chicken.

3 Cover and bake in the heated oven until the chicken is tender when pierced with the 2-pronged fork, about 1½ hours.

Conical lid of tajine seals in cooking juices and steam

TO SERVE

Taste the sauce for seasoning. Serve the chicken and sauce straight from the tajine on to individual plates.

ANNE SAYS

'If you use another type of earthenware pot or heavy casserole, be sure the lid fits tightly.'

Couscous stuffing
with almonds, used in the recipe for Stuffed Poussins with Grapes (see page 94), is the perfect accompaniment

VARIATION
MOROCCAN CHICKEN WITH AUBERGINE

1 Joint the chicken and prepare the onions and tomatoes as for Moroccan Chicken Baked with Spices.
2 Cut 1 medium aubergine (about 250 g/8 oz) in half and slice it. Put the slices in a colander, sprinkle with coarse salt, press down with a plate and leave to drain 30 minutes; wipe the slices dry with kitchen paper.
3 Trim the ends from 1 lemon and cut it into wedges.
4 Put the chicken pieces in a heavy casserole and cover with the sliced onions, chopped tomatoes, aubergine and lemon wedges.
5 In a bowl, mix together the chopped onions, 1 garlic clove, finely chopped, 125 ml (4 fl oz) olive oil, 10 ml (2 tsp) ground cumin, 10 ml (2 tsp) ground coriander, salt, pepper and a few sprigs of fresh coriander (cilantro), finely chopped. Spoon this mixture over the chicken in the casserole.
6 Sprinkle 90 g (3 oz) whole stoned black or green olives over the chicken and cook as directed. Remove the lemon wedges before serving.

INDONESIAN CHICKEN KEBABS

Saté Ayam, Bumbu Saté

🍽 SERVES 6 AS A MAIN COURSE   🥣 WORK TIME 15-20 MINUTES*   ☕ COOKING TIME 8-10 MINUTES

EQUIPMENT

food processor**

frying pan

chef's knife

pastry brush   boning knife

wooden spoon

metal spoons

rubber spatula

chopping board

bowls

18 bamboo skewers***

cling film

medium saucepan

shallow dish

***metal skewers can also be used
**blender can also be used

These spicy kebabs are sold from roadside stalls in Indonesia, where they are considered snacks, but several can be consumed as a main course with sweet, spicy peanut sauce and a salad.

* plus 3-12 hours marinating time

metric	SHOPPING LIST	imperial
1.5 kg	skinless, boneless chicken breasts	3 ½ lb
	For the marinade	
3	shallots	3
2	garlic cloves	2
2.5 ml	chilli powder	½ tsp
10 ml	ground coriander	2 tsp
10 ml	ground ginger	2 tsp
45 ml	soy sauce	3 tbsp
30 ml	distilled white vinegar	2 tbsp
30 ml	vegetable oil	2 tbsp
	For the peanut sauce	
20 ml	vegetable oil	1 ½ tbsp
175 g	shelled, skinned raw peanuts	6 oz
½	medium onion	½
1	garlic clove	1
2.5 ml	dried hot red pepper flakes	½ tsp
10 ml	ground ginger	2 tsp
5 ml	brown sugar	1 tsp
20 ml	lemon juice	1 ½ tbsp
375 ml	hot water	12 fl oz
	salt and pepper	

INGREDIENTS

chicken breasts   shallots

garlic cloves

onion   soy sauce

shelled, skinned raw peanuts   lemon juice

ground coriander   chilli powder   ground ginger

dried hot red pepper flakes   brown sugar

vegetable oil   distilled white vinegar

ORDER OF WORK

1 PREPARE AND MARINATE THE CHICKEN

2 MAKE THE PEANUT SAUCE

3 PREPARE AND COOK THE KEBABS

1 PREPARE AND MARINATE THE CHICKEN

1 Remove the tendon from each chicken breast. Separate the fillet from each breast by lifting the end of the fillet and pulling it towards you. With the chef's knife, cut each fillet in half lengthwise. Cut each breast into 7 thin strips on the diagonal, the same size as the strips of fillet.

2 Finely chop the shallots (see box, right). Finely chop the garlic. Put all the marinade ingredients in a large bowl. Mix together with a metal spoon.

Marinade ingredients give delicious flavour and moistness to chicken

3 Add the chicken strips and mix until well coated with the marinade. Cover with cling film and refrigerate at least 3 hours or up to 12 hours.

HOW TO CHOP A SHALLOT

1 If necessary, separate the shallot into sections at the root. Peel each section and set it flat side down on a chopping board. Holding the shallot steady with your fingers, slice it horizontally towards the root, leaving the slices attached at the root end. For a standard chop, slice about 3 mm (⅛ inch) thick; for a fine chop, slice as thinly as possible.

2 Slice vertically through the shallot, again leaving the root end uncut.

3 Cut across the shallot to make fine dice. Continue chopping the shallot until very fine, if necessary. The root end may be reserved for stock.

2 MAKE THE PEANUT SAUCE

1 Heat the oil in the frying pan. Add the peanuts and cook, stirring constantly, until browned, 3-5 minutes. Transfer the peanuts to the food processor.

Toast peanuts to enhance their nutty flavour

Stir nuts while browning so they do not stick and burn

2 Cut the onion into pieces and add to the food processor with the garlic, hot pepper flakes, ginger, brown sugar and lemon juice. Purée the mixture until very smooth, scraping the bowl with the spatula as necessary.

ANNE SAYS
'If the mixture is difficult to process smoothly, add a little hot water.'

3 Blend in the hot water, adding enough to make a pourable sauce. Transfer the sauce to the saucepan, heat to boiling and simmer 2 minutes, stirring constantly. Season to taste. Remove from the heat and keep warm.

! TAKE CARE !
The sauce scorches easily, so stir it all the time.

3 PREPARE AND COOK THE KEBABS

1 About 30 minutes before cooking, soak the bamboo skewers. Heat the grill. Thread the chicken strips on to the skewers concertina fashion, using 3 strips per skewer and twisting the strips slightly as you thread them.

Hold skewer steady as you twist chicken strip slightly

Thread chicken strips on to skewers in concertina fashion

To soak bamboo skewers
Cover them with cold water and allow to soak 30 minutes, then drain them.

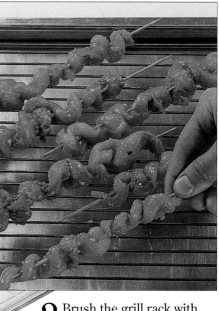

2 Brush the grill rack with oil. Arrange the chicken kebabs on the rack.

3 Grill the kebabs, about 5-7 cm (2-3 inches) from the heat until browned, 2-3 minutes. Turn and brown the other side, 2-3 minutes.

TO SERVE

Arrange the kebabs on individual plates and serve with the warm peanut sauce. Accompany with a rice pilaf for a more substantial meal.

Raw vegetable salad – shredded carrot and cabbage, sliced cucumber and tomato dressed with mild vinegar – is an excellent accompaniment for saté

VARIATION

VIETNAMESE CHICKEN KEBABS

1 Prepare the chicken breasts as for Indonesian Chicken Kebabs, but cut them into 2 cm (³/₄ inch) cubes.
2 Make the marinade by mixing 3 shallots, finely chopped, 2 garlic cloves, finely chopped, 5 ml (1 tsp) seeded and finely chopped fresh green chilli, 10 ml (2 tsp) grated fresh root ginger, 45 ml (3 tbsp) soy sauce, and 30 ml (2 tbsp) each distilled white vinegar and vegetable oil.
3 Crush 1 stalk lemon grass with a rolling pin and add to the mixture.
4 Marinate the chicken cubes 3-12 hours, then thread on to 12 soaked bamboo skewers. Discard the lemon grass.
5 Grill the kebabs as before, and serve with the peanut sauce.

— **GETTING AHEAD** —
The peanut sauce can be made up to 2 weeks ahead and kept, covered, in the refrigerator. The chicken can be left to marinate 12 hours, but do not cook until just before serving.

CHICKEN IN RED WINE

Coq au Vin

 SERVES 4-6　 WORK TIME 30 MINUTES*　 COOKING TIME 1½-1¾ HOURS

EQUIPMENT

chef's knife

small knife

bowls

small ladle

medium saucepan

slotted spoon

wooden spoon

2-pronged fork

kitchen paper

platter

large flameproof casserole with lid

sieve

cling film

conical sieve

chopping board

ANNE SAYS

'This dish varies with the wine used – a Rhône wine gives a rich dark sauce, a Loire wine a more fruity result. Personally, I like a full-bodied red Burgundy.'

In this classic dish, the bird is marinated to tenderise and give it flavour, then simmered in a red wine sauce and served with a garnish of diced-bacon, baby onions and mushrooms.
The more mature the chicken, the better the dish will be – French cooks use a boiling fowl or, best of all, the traditional male cock bird.

*plus 12-18 hours marinating time

metric	SHOPPING LIST	imperial
2 kg	chicken	4 ½ lb
125 g	piece of bacon	4 oz
15 ml	vegetable oil	1 tbsp
15 g	butter	½ oz
18-20	baby onions	18-20
250 g	mushrooms	8 oz
1	garlic clove	1
2	shallots	2
45 ml	flour	3 tbsp
500 ml	chicken stock or water	16 fl oz
1	bouquet garni	1
	salt and pepper	
	For the marinade	
1	onion	1
1	celery stick	1
1	carrot	1
1	garlic clove	1
6	black peppercorns	6
375 ml	red Burgundy wine	12 fl oz
30 ml	olive oil	2 tbsp

INGREDIENTS

carrot

butter

piece of bacon

chicken

mushrooms

onion

garlic cloves

red wine

celery stick

baby onions

bouquet garni

shallots

flour

olive oil

black peppercorns

chicken stock

vegetable oil

ORDER OF WORK

1. **JOINT AND MARINATE THE CHICKEN**

2. **SAUTE THE CHICKEN**

3. **PREPARE THE GARNISH**

4. **FINISH THE COOKING**

HOW TO JOINT A CHICKEN INTO 8 PIECES

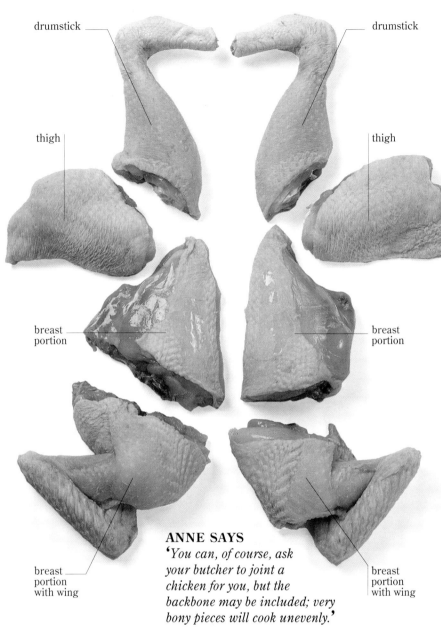

drumstick

drumstick

thigh

thigh

breast portion

breast portion

breast portion with wing

breast portion with wing

ANNE SAYS

'You can, of course, ask your butcher to joint a chicken for you, but the backbone may be included; very bony pieces will cook unevenly.'

1 Using a chef's knife, cut down between the leg joint and body on one side. Twist the bone sharply outwards to break the joint, then cut through it and pull the leg from the body. Repeat this procedure for the other leg.

2 Slit closely along both sides of the breastbone to loosen the meat, then split the breastbone. Turn the bird over on to its breast and cut along one side of the backbone. The bird is now divided in half.

ANNE SAYS

'You can use poultry shears instead of a chef's knife, if you prefer; they are especially good for splitting the breastbone, cutting the backbone and rib bones, and cutting the breast and legs in half.'

3 Cut the backbone and rib bones in one piece from the breast where they are still attached, leaving the wing joints attached to the breast.

4 Cut each breast piece in half diagonally, cutting through the breast and rib bones so that a portion of the breast meat is cut off with the wing. Cut off any sharp bones.

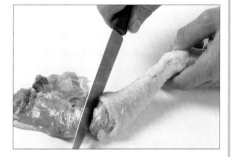

5 Cut each leg in half through the joint, between the thigh and the drumstick, using the line of fat as a guide.

1 JOINT AND MARINATE THE CHICKEN

1 To make the marinade, thinly slice the onion. Trim and thinly slice the celery. Thinly slice the carrot.

2 Put the onion, celery, carrot, garlic clove and peppercorns in the saucepan. Pour in the red wine and bring to the boil. Simmer 5 minutes, then allow to cool completely.

3 Joint the chicken into 8 pieces (see box, page 29). Put the chicken pieces in a bowl, pour over the cooled marinade, then spoon the olive oil on top. Cover with cling film and leave the chicken to marinate 12-18 hours in the refrigerator, turning the pieces occasionally.

Use bowl sieve with legs to free your hands for other chores

Marinating liquid and vegetables will be added separately

4 Remove the chicken pieces from the marinade and pat them dry thoroughly with kitchen paper.

5 Strain the marinade through the sieve over a bowl and reserve both the liquid and the vegetables.

2 SAUTE THE CHICKEN

1 Dice the bacon. Heat the oil and butter in the casserole until foaming, add the bacon and fry until browned and the fat is extracted. Remove the bacon with the slotted spoon and reserve it.

2 Add the chicken pieces to the casserole, skin side down, and cook until well browned, about 10 minutes.

3 Turn the chicken pieces over and brown the other side, then remove them.

Use long-pronged fork to protect your fingers from sizzling fat

HOW TO CLEAN AND QUARTER OR SLICE MUSHROOMS

1 Trim the stalk from each mushroom just level with the cap. Wipe the mushrooms clean with damp kitchen paper. If they are dirty, swirl them in a bowl of cold water; drain in a colander.

2 **To quarter mushrooms:** hold each mushroom on the chopping board stalk side down and cut into quarters.

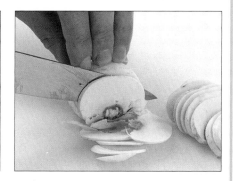

To slice mushrooms: hold each mushroom stalk side down and cut vertically into slices of the required thickness.

3 PREPARE THE GARNISH

1 Put the baby onions in a bowl, cover with hot water and leave 2 minutes. Remove the onions and peel them.

Immerse onions in hot water to loosen skins

2 Clean the mushrooms and cut them into quarters (see box, page 31). Chop the garlic. Chop the shallots.

3 Add the baby onions to the casserole and sauté lightly until browned. Lift out with the slotted spoon and reserve. Add the mushrooms and sauté until tender, 2-3 minutes. Remove the mushrooms with the slotted spoon and reserve.

4 FINISH THE COOKING

1 Discard all but about 30 ml (2 tbsp) of the fat from the casserole and add the reserved vegetables from the marinade. Cook over very low heat until softened, 5 minutes. Sprinkle the flour over the vegetables and cook, stirring, until lightly browned, 2-3 minutes.

2 Stir in the reserved marinade and the chicken stock and add the chopped garlic and shallots, the bouquet garni, salt and pepper. Heat until boiling, stirring well.

Use small ladle to press sauce through sieve

3 Replace the chicken pieces, cover and simmer over low heat until the pieces are just tender when pierced with the 2-pronged fork, 45-60 minutes. Transfer the chicken pieces to a plate and keep warm; pour the sauce into a bowl.

4 Wipe out the casserole and add the baby onions. Strain the sauce over them through the conical sieve, pressing down on the vegetables with the small ladle to extract the maximum flavour and liquid.

5 Simmer over low heat until the onions are almost tender, 5-10 minutes. Add the mushrooms and continue to simmer until the sauce is reduced and lightly coats the back of a spoon, 2-3 minutes longer. Taste for seasoning.

Sauce should adhere but not be too thick

6 Add the chicken pieces and bacon to the sauce and reheat gently 3-4 minutes.

🍴 TO SERVE
Spoon the chicken and sauce from the casserole on to warmed individual plates. Serve with steamed baby potatoes or potatoes fried in butter and oil.

VARIATIONS

CHICKEN IN WHITE WINE
Coq au Vin Blanc

Prepare as for Chicken in Red Wine, but omit the bacon and replace the red wine in the marinade with an equal quantity of medium-dry white wine, such as a Riesling.

CHICKEN IN BEAUJOLAIS
Coq au Beaujolais
A lighter version of the classic Coq au Vin.

Prepare as for Chicken in Red Wine, but omit the bacon and mushrooms and replace the Burgundy red wine with an equal quantity of fruity red Beaujolais.

GETTING AHEAD
Chicken in Red Wine can be prepared up to 2 days ahead and kept, covered, in the refrigerator (the flavour will mature). Reheat it gently on the stove.

TEX-MEX CHICKEN SALAD

¶O¶ SERVES 4-6 ⊕ WORK TIME 20-25 MINUTES

EQUIPMENT

bowls

chopping board

small knife

chef's knife

boning knife

metal spoon

rubber gloves

whisk

forks

salad spinner

ANNE SAYS

'If you don't have a salad spinner, pat the washed lettuce dry with kitchen paper or a clean tea towel.'

This tasty chicken salad is a meal in itself. Mexican tortilla chips are the best accompaniment, but a loaf of crusty French bread or wholewheat rolls would go equally well.

GETTING AHEAD

The chicken can be roasted 2 or 3 days in advance and kept, well wrapped, in the refrigerator. The vinaigrette dressing can be prepared up to 1 week in advance and kept in a sealed jar or bottle at room temperature. Simply add the fresh tarragon just before serving.

metric	SHOPPING LIST	imperial
1.8 kg	whole cooked chicken	4 lb
	or 500 g (1 lb) cooked skinless, boneless chicken	
1-2	fresh chillies, to taste	1-2
2	large tomatoes	2
1	red pepper	1
1	shallot	1
500 g	large Cos or Little Gem lettuce	1 lb
175 g	drained canned sweetcorn	6 oz
	For the vinaigrette dressing	
60 ml	red wine vinegar	4 tbsp
10 ml	Dijon mustard	2 tsp
2.5 ml	salt	½ tsp
1.25 ml	pepper	¼ tsp
175 ml	vegetable oil	6 fl oz
3	sprigs of fresh tarragon	3

INGREDIENTS

whole cooked chicken

red pepper

shallot

sweetcorn

chillies

tomatoes

fresh tarragon

Cos lettuce

 Dijon mustard

vegetable oil

red wine vinegar

ORDER OF WORK

1 PREPARE THE SALAD INGREDIENTS

2 ASSEMBLE THE SALAD

1 PREPARE THE SALAD INGREDIENTS

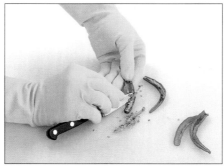

Cut lettuce rolls across into strips

1 If using a whole cooked chicken, remove the meat from the bones, discarding all skin and any gristle. With the chef's knife, cut the chicken meat into thin slices.

ANNE SAYS
'You should have about 500 g (1 lb) of chicken meat in slices.'

2 With the small knife, cut the stalk from the chilli and halve the chilli lengthwise. Scrape out the chilli seeds and the inner white core.

! TAKE CARE !
When handling chillies, always wear rubber gloves to protect your hands from the alkaloid, capsaicin, which may irritate your skin.

3 Put one chilli half on top of the other and slice thinly, then chop the slices into a fine dice.

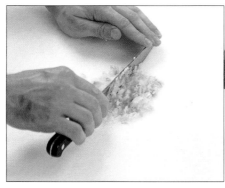

4 Remove the cores from the tomatoes. With the chef's knife, cut the tomatoes into thin slices.

5 Core, seed and dice the red pepper (see box, below). Finely chop the shallot.

6 Pull the lettuce leaves from the core. Wash the leaves, then dry in the salad spinner. Stack 3 or 4 leaves and roll tightly. Slice into strips.

HOW TO CORE, SEED AND DICE A PEPPER

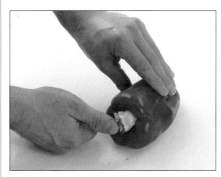

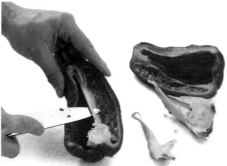

1 Cut around the pepper core, twist and pull it out.

2 Halve the pepper. Cut away the protruding ribs and scrape out the seeds. Rinse the pepper under cold running water and pat dry.

3 Cut each pepper half lengthwise into thin strips, then cut the strips across into a fine dice.

HOW TO MAKE VINAIGRETTE DRESSING

1 Put the vinegar, mustard, salt and pepper in a small bowl and whisk to combine thoroughly and dissolve the salt.

2 Add the oil in a thin stream, whisking constantly so that the dressing emulsifies and thickens slightly.

3 Finely chop the tarragon. Stir the tarragon into the dressing and taste for seasoning.

ANNE SAYS
'*Vinaigrette will last up to 1 week in a sealed jar or bottle. The dressing will separate but a brisk shake will re-emulsify the ingredients. Store at room temperature because some oils solidify when chilled. Add flavourings (shallots, herbs or garlic) at the last minute so flavour is fresh.*'

2 ASSEMBLE THE SALAD

1 Make the vinaigrette dressing (see box, left). Combine the chicken and shallot in a large bowl with 45-60 ml (3-4 tbsp) of the dressing.

2 Put the lettuce in another large bowl. Add 45-60 ml (3-4 tbsp) of the vinaigrette dressing and toss.

3 Arrange the lettuce on individual plates and mound the chicken on top. Arrange the tomatoes around the edges of the plates and spoon the sweetcorn on top of the tomatoes. Scatter the red pepper on top of the chicken and drizzle over the remaining vinaigrette.

4 With a fork, sprinkle lightly with the chopped chilli and serve.

Tortilla chips are an excellent accompaniment for the salad, providing a crunchy contrast to the chicken and vegetables

Roquefort, or any blue cheese, adds sharp flavour

Bacon adds crisp texture

VARIATION

COBB SALAD

A California classic with a striking variety of colours.

1 Prepare the chicken, shallot, lettuce, tomatoes and vinaigrette dressing as for the Tex-Mex Salad (omitting the red pepper, fresh chillies and sweetcorn).

2 Stack 6 rashers of bacon (total weight about 175 g/6 oz) and cut crosswise into 1 cm (½ inch) strips. In a small frying pan, cook the bacon until browned. Drain on kitchen paper.

3 Crumble 90 g (3 oz) Roquefort or other blue cheese.

4 Prepare and slice 2 avocados (see box, below).

5 Assemble the salad, sprinkling on lemon juice as necessary to prevent the avocados from discolouring, and serve.

HOW TO PREPARE AND SLICE AN AVOCADO

1 With a chef's knife, cut lengthwise around the avocado to the stone. Twist to loosen and separate the halves, then pull them apart.

2 Embed the blade of the knife in the stone and twist gently to remove. Alternatively, scoop out the stone with a spoon.

3 With a small knife, make a shallow incision in the skin of each avocado half, taking care not to cut into the flesh. Peel the skin.

4 Cut the avocado halves lengthwise into thin slices. Lay them on a plate and sprinkle with lemon juice to prevent discolouring.

! TAKE CARE !
Use a stainless steel knife when slicing avocados to prevent the flesh from discolouring.

SAUTE OF CHICKEN WITH PAPRIKA

 SERVES 4 WORK TIME 20-25 MINUTES COOKING TIME 40-50 MINUTES

EQUIPMENT

 chef's knife

 small knife

plastic bag

chopping board

small bowl

large sauté pan with lid

2-pronged fork

wooden spoon

shallow dish

The basic sauté technique involves browning the chicken in fat, then cooking it in its own juices, with an addition of either water, stock or wine. Onion is almost always included among the flavourings, but there is no end to the variety of garnishes and sauces for sautéed chicken. This Hungarian-style version is just one example.

GETTING AHEAD

The sautéed chicken, and the sauce prepared up to the end of step 2, can be made up to 2 days in advance and kept, covered, in the refrigerator. Add soured cream before serving.

INGREDIENTS

 chicken

 red peppers

 onion

 butter

 soured cream

 vegetable oil

 chicken stock

 tomato purée

paprika

metric	SHOPPING LIST	imperial
1.5 kg	chicken	3 ½ lb
45 ml	paprika	3 tbsp
	salt and pepper	
1	medium onion	1
15 ml	vegetable oil	1 tbsp
15 g	butter	½ oz
250 ml	chicken stock	8 fl oz
4	medium red peppers	4
15 ml	tomato purée	1 tbsp
125 ml	soured cream	4 fl oz

ORDER OF WORK

1 SAUTE THE CHICKEN

2 MAKE THE SAUCE

1 SAUTE THE CHICKEN

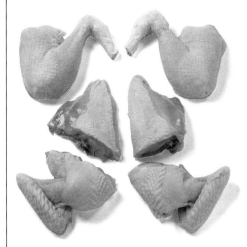

1 Joint the chicken into 6 pieces (see Steps 1-4, How to Joint a Chicken into 8 Pieces, page 29). Sprinkle the pieces with the paprika, salt and pepper, patting to coat evenly. Chop the onion (see box, below).

3 Push the chicken to one side of the pan and add the onion to the other. Stir to combine with the fat, scraping the pan, and sauté until soft but not brown, about 3 minutes. Spread out the chicken again and add half of the stock. Cover and cook until the chicken is tender, 15-25 minutes. Meanwhile, roast, seed and slice the peppers (see box, page 40).

2 Heat the oil and butter in the sauté pan over moderate heat until foaming. Add the chicken legs, skin side down, and sauté until they begin to brown, about 5 minutes. Add the breast pieces and continue cooking gently until very brown, about 10-15 minutes longer. Turn and brown the other side.

! TAKE CARE !
Do not let the paprika scorch or it will taste bitter.

4 To check if the chicken is cooked, pierce the meat with the 2-pronged fork. The juices should run clear. If some pieces cook before others, remove them and keep warm.

HOW TO CHOP AN ONION

1 Peel the onion, leaving on the root to hold the onion together. Cut the onion in half and lay one half, cut side down, on the chopping board. With a chef's knife, make a series of horizontal cuts from the stalk towards the root. Cut just to the root of the onion but not through it.

2 Make a series of lengthwise vertical cuts, cutting just to the root but not through it.

ANNE SAYS
'When slicing, tuck your fingertips under and use your knuckles to guide the blade of the knife.'

3 Slice the onion crosswise into dice. (Adjust the distance between the slices depending on whether you want it coarse or fine. For finely chopped onion, continue chopping until you have the fineness required for the recipe.)

HOW TO ROAST, SEED AND SLICE A PEPPER

1 Roast the pepper under the grill, turning as needed, until the skin is black and blistered, 10-12 minutes. Alternatively, hold the pepper with a 2-pronged fork over a gas flame until the skin is charred. Immediately put the pepper in a plastic bag, close it and allow to cool (steam trapped inside helps loosen the skin). Peel off skin.

2 Cut around the pepper core and pull it out. Halve the pepper and scrape out the seeds with the knife. Rinse the pepper and pat dry.

3 With a chef's knife, cut each pepper half lengthwise into thin strips.

2 MAKE THE SAUCE

1 Remove all the chicken pieces from the pan and keep warm. Boil the pan juices, stirring, until reduced to a shiny glaze. Stir in the tomato purée. Add the remaining stock and stir until boiling.

2 Return all the chicken pieces to the pan, add the red pepper strips to the sauce and heat through gently, 1-2 minutes.

3 Add most of the soured cream and shake the pan gently to mix it into the sauce. Taste for seasoning.

! TAKE CARE !
Do not boil the sauce after the soured cream has been added or it will curdle.

Noodles, both plain and spinach, make a cool contrast to pungent paprika sauce

🍴 TO SERVE
Arrange the chicken pieces on individual plates; spoon over the pepper strips and sauce and the remaining soured cream.

VARIATION
SAUTE OF CHICKEN WITH BEER

The pungent flavours of beer and gin replace the spice in Chicken with Paprika.

Flageolet beans, plainly boiled and tossed with butter and parsley, are a perfect accompaniment

Beer-based cream sauce contains hints of flambéed gin

1 Joint the chicken as directed, then coat the pieces with 45-60 ml (3-4 tbsp) seasoned flour in place of the paprika.
2 Sauté the chicken, adding 2 chopped onions as directed. Add 45-60 ml (3-4 tbsp) gin to the sauté pan and heat, then light carefully with a match to flame it.
3 Add stout in place of the chicken stock, season with salt and pepper, and continue cooking as directed, skimming off any excess fat at the end of cooking.
4 Omit the red peppers and tomato purée, and finish the sauce with only 60 ml (4 tbsp) soured cream.
5 Chop a few sprigs of parsley and sprinkle over the chicken before serving.
6 Flageolet beans, or broad beans, plainly boiled and tossed with a little butter and chopped parsley, are an excellent accompaniment for the chicken.

VARIATION
SZECHUAN PEPPER CHICKEN

A distant cousin of the classic Steak au Poivre, this uses aromatic Szechuan pepper rather than paprika to spice the chicken.

Wild rice is mixed with white rice for an effective garnish

1 Toast 30 g (1 oz) Szechuan pepper in a small dry pan over very low heat, tossing the pepper and shaking the pan until the pepper smells aromatic, 3-5 minutes.
2 Put the pepper in a plastic bag and crush finely with a rolling pin; alternatively, grind the pepper in a spice mill.
3 Joint the chicken as directed, then coat the pieces with the pepper in place of the paprika.
4 Sauté the chicken, adding the chopped onion and chicken stock as directed; omit the peppers.
5 To make the sauce, boil the pan juices to a shiny glaze. Add the remaining stock and boil again to a glaze; omit the tomato purée. Replace the soured cream with double cream; add it all to the pan juices and boil, stirring, until the sauce is rich and slightly thickened, 1-2 minutes. Taste for seasoning.
6 Serve with a mixture of wild and white rices.

CHICKEN EN COCOTTE WITH LEMON AND PARMESAN

🍴 SERVES 4 🥄 WORK TIME 15-20 MINUTES 🍲 COOKING TIME 45-55 MINUTES

EQUIPMENT

large flameproof casserole with lid

saucepan

poultry shears

small knife

boning knife

vegetable peeler

metal spoon

large metal spoon

2-pronged fork

trussing needle and string

whisk

kitchen paper

platter

chopping board

conical sieve

aluminium foil

small bowl

These young chickens are cooked in a covered casserole to keep them moist, then halved to make attractive serving portions. The simple cream sauce, piquant with lemon and Parmesan cheese, is made from the pan juices. Serve with a selection of crisply cooked vegetables.

GETTING AHEAD
The chickens can be cooked and kept with their pan juices, covered, in the refrigerator up to 24 hours. Reheat the chickens 20-25 minutes in a 180°C (350°F, Gas 4) oven, then make the sauce just before serving.

INGREDIENTS

chickens

lemons

butter

double cream

chicken stock

arrowroot

Parmesan cheese

metric	SHOPPING LIST	imperial
2 x 1 kg	chickens	2 x 2-2 ½ lb
	salt and pepper	
2	lemons	2
45 g	butter	1½ oz
For the cheese sauce		
125 ml	chicken stock	4 fl oz
125 ml	double cream	4 fl oz
5 ml	arrowroot	1 tsp
15 ml	water	1 tbsp
30 g	grated Parmesan cheese	1 oz

ORDER OF WORK

1 COOK THE CHICKENS

2 MAKE THE CHEESE SAUCE

3 CUT THE CHICKENS IN HALF FOR SERVING

HOW TO TRUSS A CHICKEN

1 Wipe the inside of the chicken with kitchen paper and season it inside and out with salt and pepper.

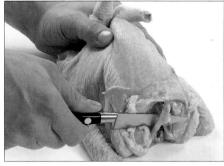

2 With a small knife, remove the wishbone.

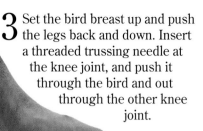

3 Set the bird breast up and push the legs back and down. Insert a threaded trussing needle at the knee joint, and push it through the bird and out through the other knee joint.

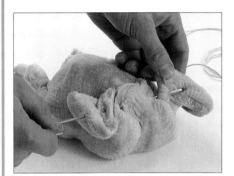

4 Turn the bird over so it is breast down. Pull the neck skin over the neck cavity and tuck the wing tips over it. Push the needle through both sections of one wing and into the neck skin. Continue under the backbone of the bird to the other side. Push the needle through the second wing in the same way, through both wing bones.

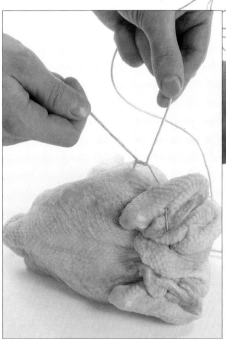

Hold both feet steady with one hand

5 Turn the bird on to its side. Pull the ends of the string firmly together and tie them securely. Turn the bird breast up. Tuck the tail into the cavity of the bird and fold over the top skin. Push the needle through the skin.

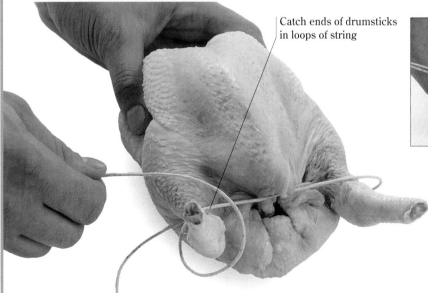

Catch ends of drumsticks in loops of string

6 Loop the string around one drumstick, under the breastbone and over the other drumstick. Tie the ends of the string together.

ANNE SAYS
'Chickens hold a better shape and are easier to carve if you truss them.'

1 COOK THE CHICKENS

1 Heat the oven to 190°C (375°F, Gas 5). Truss the chickens (see box, page 43). Pare the zest from the lemons with the vegetable peeler.

2 Melt the butter in the casserole. Add one chicken and brown it on all sides, 5-10 minutes. Transfer it to the platter and brown the second chicken.

3 Return the first chicken to the casserole. Add the lemon zest and cover the casserole. Cook the chickens in the heated oven, turning them occasionally so they cook evenly.

ANNE SAYS
'*Instead of pot roasting in the oven, the chickens can be cooked on top of the stove over low heat.*'

Scatter zest over both chickens

4 After 30-40 minutes, lift the birds with the 2-pronged fork. The juices that run out should not be pink. Transfer the birds to the board, cover with foil and keep them warm.

2 MAKE THE CHEESE SAUCE

Sit sieve securely in or on saucepan so you have both hands free to hold casserole

1 Remove the excess fat from the casserole and discard. Add the stock and bring to the boil, stirring to dissolve the pan juices.

2 Boil the stock until well reduced, about 5 minutes. Strain it into the saucepan.

3 Add the cream and whisk to mix, then bring just to the boil.

4 Stir the arrowroot and water together in the small bowl to form a smooth paste. Whisk in enough of the arrowroot paste to thicken the sauce. It should lightly coat the back of a spoon.

Whisk enough arrowroot paste into sauce to thicken to desired consistency

5 Take the sauce from the heat and whisk in the Parmesan cheese. Taste for seasoning. Keep warm.

! TAKE CARE !

Do not reboil the sauce or the cheese may cook into strings.

3 CUT THE CHICKENS IN HALF FOR SERVING

Hold chicken securely with 2-pronged fork

Poultry shears cut through breastbone more easily than sharp knife

1 Discard the trussing strings from the chickens. Set a bird breast up on the board. Slice closely along the breastbone with the boning knife to loosen the meat.

2 Cut along one side of the breastbone with poultry shears. Turn the bird over; cut along each side of the backbone and discard it. Repeat with the other bird.

¶●¶ TO SERVE
Set each chicken half on an individual serving plate and spoon over the sauce.

Crisp stir-fried vegetables complement the lightly sauced chicken perfectly

Half a young chicken makes an ideal serving for one, giving both white and dark meat

Creamy sauce has rich tang of Parmesan cheese

CHICKEN WITH THYME

Sprigs of fresh thyme delicately scent the chicken in this dish in place of the lemon zest.

1 Omit the lemon from the main recipe and cook the chicken with 4-5 sprigs of fresh thyme instead.
2 Make the cream sauce but do not add cheese.
3 Garnish the chicken with finely chopped fresh thyme, sprinkling it on in neat, curved lines, if you like. Broccoli florets and thin sticks of courgette make good accompaniments.

CHICKEN EN COCOTTE WITH JUNIPER BERRIES AND WILD MUSHROOMS

The earthy combination of juniper berries and wild mushrooms is ideal with chicken.

1 With a rolling pin, coarsely crush 30-45 ml (2-3 tbsp) juniper berries in a thick plastic bag.
2 Omit the lemon from the main recipe and add the juniper berries instead; cook as directed.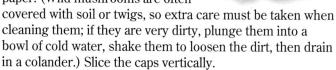
3 Trim the stalks from 250 g (8 oz) fresh wild mushrooms such as shiitake or chanterelles, then clean them with damp kitchen paper. (Wild mushrooms are often covered with soil or twigs, so extra care must be taken when cleaning them; if they are very dirty, plunge them into a bowl of cold water, shake them to loosen the dirt, then drain in a colander.) Slice the caps vertically.
4 In a frying pan, sauté the mushrooms in 30 g (1 oz) butter with salt and pepper until softened.
5 Make the cream sauce but do not add cheese; stir the sautéed mushrooms into the sauce after it has thickened.

GRILLED CHICKEN THIGHS IN YOGURT

 SERVES 4 WORK TIME 20-25 MINUTES* COOKING TIME 15-20 MINUTES

EQUIPMENT

kitchen paper

food processor**

platter

pastry brush

chef's knife

palette knife

2-pronged fork

wooden spoon

chopping board

small saucepan

grill pan and rack

large bowl

**blender can also be used

In this Middle Eastern-style recipe, plain yogurt plays a double role: first it tenderises the chicken, then it helps thicken and enrich the sauce. During the summer months, stoke up your barbecue and grill the chicken outdoors. The chicken thighs and coriander sauce can be served hot or at room temperature.

GETTING AHEAD

The sauce can be prepared up to 24 hours ahead and kept, covered, in the refrigerator. Reheat it gently so that it does not boil and separate. The chicken can be marinated up to 24 hours, but grill it at the last minute.

* plus 3-4 hours marinating time

INGREDIENTS

garlic cloves

chicken thighs

onion

fresh coriander

ground coriander

plain yogurt

soured cream

vegetable oil

metric	SHOPPING LIST	imperial
8	chicken thighs	8
250 ml	plain yogurt	8 fl oz
	salt and pepper	
	vegetable oil for grill rack	
	For the coriander sauce	
1	medium onion	1
2	garlic cloves	2
30 ml	vegetable oil	2 tbsp
30 ml	ground coriander	2 tbsp
250 ml	plain yogurt	8 fl oz
a few	sprigs of fresh coriander	a few
125 ml	soured cream	4 fl oz

ORDER OF WORK

1 PREPARE THE CHICKEN

2 COOK THE CHICKEN

3 MAKE THE CORIANDER SAUCE

1 PREPARE THE CHICKEN

1 Put the chicken thighs in the large bowl and pour over the plain yogurt. Season the yogurt with salt and pepper to taste.

Stir yogurt to make it smooth before pouring

2 Turn the chicken thighs with your hands until the chicken is well coated with yogurt, then cover the bowl tightly and set aside to marinate in the refrigerator, 3-4 hours.

3 Heat the grill. Brush the rack in the grill pan with oil. Lift the chicken pieces out of the bowl. With the palette knife, scrape off the yogurt, discarding it.

Use palette knife to spread coating evenly

4 Dry the chicken pieces with kitchen paper, then arrange them on the oiled grill rack.

HOW TO PEEL AND CHOP GARLIC

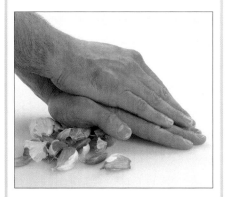

1 To separate the garlic cloves, crush the bulb with the palms of your hands, putting one on top of the other to exert pressure. Alternatively, pull a clove from the bulb with your fingers.

2 To peel the clove, lightly crush it with the flat of a chef's knife to loosen the skin. Peel off the skin with your fingers.

3 Set the flat side of the knife on top of the clove and strike with your fist. Finely chop the garlic with the knife, rocking the blade back and forth.

2 COOK THE CHICKEN

1 Grill the chicken thighs, about 7.5 cm (3 inches) from the heat, until the tops are very brown, about 8-10 minutes. Turn the pieces over.

2 Continue grilling until the pieces are very brown and no pink juice runs out when they are pierced with the 2-pronged fork, 7-10 minutes longer. While the chicken is cooking, make the sauce.

3 MAKE THE CORIANDER SAUCE

1 Chop the onion. Finely chop the garlic (see box, left). Heat the oil in the saucepan and sauté the onion until soft and starting to brown.

Ground coriander adds deliciously sweet and pungent taste

2 Add the ground coriander and garlic and continue cooking over low heat for 2-3 minutes, stirring constantly.

3 Purée the onion mixture with the yogurt in the food processor. Add the fresh coriander and process just until it is chopped.

4 Return to the saucepan. Pour in the soured cream, then season with salt and pepper. Heat the sauce, stirring constantly. Taste for seasoning and keep warm.

! TAKE CARE !
When heating a sauce that contains yogurt or soured cream, do not let it boil or it will separate.

TO SERVE
Arrange 2 chicken thighs on each warmed plate and spoon the sauce around them.

Fresh mint sprigs
add colour to
finished dish

Tabouleh salad
is refreshing
accompaniment to
spicy chicken thighs

V A R I A T I O N

GRILLED CHICKEN THIGHS WITH YOGURT AND HONEY

1 Marinate the chicken as for Grilled Chicken Thighs in Yogurt, adding 30 ml (2 tbsp) honey and 5 ml (1 tsp) ground ginger to the yogurt.
2 Meanwhile, spread 60 g (2 oz) pine nuts on a baking sheet and bake in a 190° C (375° F, Gas 5) oven until evenly browned, 5-8 minutes; set aside.
3 Grill the chicken as directed, without scraping off the yogurt mixture and brushing with the excess yogurt mixture several times during cooking.
4 While the chicken is cooking, prepare the sauce as directed in the recipe for Grilled Chicken Thighs in Yogurt, omitting the ground and fresh coriander. After the sauce has been puréed, stir in the soured cream and 75 g (2 ½ oz) raisins and heat as directed.
5 Arrange the chicken on individual plates and sprinkle over the toasted pine nuts.
6 Serve the sauce separately or in lettuce cups as shown above.
7 A green salad is also a good accompaniment.

CHICKEN POJARSKI

Kuritsa Pojarski

🍽 SERVES 4   🥣 WORK TIME 35-40 MINUTES   🍲 COOKING TIME 40-50 MINUTES

EQUIPMENT

deep-fat fryer

deep-fat thermometer if needed

medium sauté pan

chef's knife

boning knife

small frying pan

baking sheet

slotted spoon

palette knife

chopping board

wooden spoon

small ladle   pastry brush

metal skewers

shallow dishes

bowls

aluminium foil

mincer*

conical sieve

*food processor can also be used

INGREDIENTS

chicken breasts

brioches

bouquet garni

tomatoes

mushrooms

onion

garlic clove

seasoned flour

sugar

egg

milk

double cream

tomato purée

oil for deep frying

vegetable oil

ground nutmeg

This dish is a variation of the traditional pojarski, *once a favourite of the Russian royal family.*

GETTING AHEAD

The *pojarski* can be prepared up to the end of step 2, then refrigerated up to 12 hours. The sauce can be made and kept, covered, in the refrigerator up to 3 days.

metric	SHOPPING LIST	imperial
6	individual brioches, total weight about 250 g (8 oz)	6
125 ml	milk	4 fl oz
420 g	skinless, boneless chicken breasts	14 oz
45 ml	double cream	3 tbsp
	ground nutmeg	
	salt and pepper	
30 g	seasoned flour	1 oz
1	egg	1
	oil for deep frying	
For the tomato and mushroom sauce		
500 g	tomatoes	1 lb
1	small onion	1
1	garlic clove	1
125 g	mushrooms	4 oz
30 ml	vegetable oil	2 tbsp
15 ml	tomato purée	1 tbsp
1	bouquet garni	1
	sugar	

ORDER OF WORK

1 PREPARE THE CHICKEN MIXTURE

2 SHAPE AND COOK THE POJARSKI

3 MAKE THE TOMATO AND MUSHROOM SAUCE

1 PREPARE THE CHICKEN MIXTURE

1 Cut 4 of the brioches into dice, using the chef's knife, and set aside. Break apart the remaining brioches and put them in a small bowl.

Challah, egg bread or ordinary white bread can be substituted for brioche

2 Pour the milk over the brioches in the bowl and soak for 5 minutes. Squeeze any excess milk from the soaked brioches.

3 Remove the tendon from each chicken breast (see box, below). Cut the chicken into chunks. Work it through the fine blade of the mincer with the soaked brioches.

HOW TO REMOVE THE TENDON FROM A CHICKEN BREAST

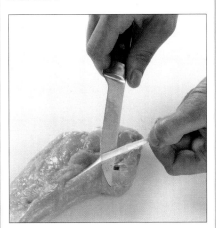

Strip the tendon from the centre of the breast, stroking it with a boning knife to remove it cleanly. If the inner fillet becomes detached from the rest of the breast meat, replace it.

ANNE SAYS
'*A food processor can also be used, but take care not to purée the meat too finely.*'

4 With the wooden spoon, beat the cream into the minced chicken mixture with a pinch of nutmeg and salt and pepper.

5 To test the mixture for seasoning, fry a little piece in the frying pan and taste – it should be well seasoned, so add more salt and pepper if required.

2 SHAPE AND COOK THE POJARSKI

1 With wet hands, shape the mixture into 4 balls and flatten slightly. Dip them in the seasoned flour and pat off the excess to obtain an even coating. Beat the egg and brush on to the rounds, draining off any excess.

2 Coat rounds in diced brioches, patting so they are completely covered. Chill, uncovered, in the refrigerator about 30 minutes.

Fry pojarski in batches so they are not crowded in pan

3 Heat the oven to 190°C (375°F, Gas 5). Heat the oil in the deep-fat fryer to 180°C (350°F). Add 1-2 of the pojarski to the oil and fry until brown, 2-3 minutes.

ANNE SAYS
'To test the oil temperature without a thermometer, drop in a cube of bread: it should turn golden brown in 1 minute.'

Use skewer to check that pojarski are cooked all the way through

4 With the slotted spoon, transfer the pojarski to the baking sheet as they are fried. Fry the remaining pojarski in the same way.

5 Bake the pojarski in the heated oven until the skewer inserted in the centre is hot to the touch when withdrawn, 25-30 minutes. If they seem to be browning too quickly, cover them loosely with foil. While they are in the oven, make the sauce.

3 MAKE THE TOMATO AND MUSHROOM SAUCE

1 Chop the tomatoes. Chop the onion. Chop the garlic. Slice the mushrooms.

Press down well on tomato mixture

2 Heat half of the vegetable oil in the sauté pan, add the onion and cook until browned, 2-3 minutes. Stir in the tomatoes, tomato purée, garlic, bouquet garni, salt, pepper and a pinch of sugar and cook, stirring occasionally, until fairly thick, 8-10 minutes.

3 Press the tomato mixture through the sieve into a bowl, using the small ladle and pressing down to extract all the pulp.

🍴 TO SERVE

Put pojarski on warmed plates and spoon sauce around. Serve with an earthy accompaniment such as kasha (buckwheat grains).

4 Wipe out the sauté pan, heat the remaining oil and sauté the mushrooms until tender, without letting them brown. Stir in the tomato mixture and taste for seasoning.

V A R I A T I O N

COCKTAIL POJARSKI

These small balls are ideal finger food for parties. Serve them garnished with salad leaves and black olives.

1 In the main recipe, cut the brioches into small dice and shape the chicken mixture into 2.5 cm (1 inch) balls.
2 Proceed as directed; the small pojarski will need only 5-10 minutes baking in the oven.
3 Serve on cocktail sticks without the sauce.

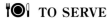

Fresh herbs or salad leaves are an attractive garnish

SAUTE OF CHICKEN WITH MUSSELS

🍽️ SERVES 4 ⌁ WORK TIME 30-35 MINUTES ♨ COOKING TIME 40-50 MINUTES

EQUIPMENT

stiff brush

small knife

large sauté pan with lid

colander

chef's knife

2-pronged fork

slotted spoon

wooden spoon

large saucepan

shallow dish

chopping board

aluminium foil

Seasoned flour *is used for coating food to be sautéed or deep fried. Mix 30 g (1 oz) flour, 5 ml (1 tsp) salt and 2.5 ml (½ tsp) pepper to coat a 1.5-1.8 kg (3½-4 lb) chicken, jointed.*

The combination of mussels and chicken may sound unusual, but it's quite delicious, a distant cousin of paella. Juice from the steamed mussels adds an intense flavour to the dish. The orange meat of the mussels in their blue-black shells and the fresh green of chives and tender-crisp beans make a colourful presentation.

GETTING AHEAD

The chicken can be sautéed up to the end of step 4 and then refrigerated, covered, in the wine sauce up to 2 days. The beans and mussels are best prepared just before finishing the dish.

metric	SHOPPING LIST	imperial
1.5 kg	chicken	3½ lb
30 g	seasoned flour (see box, left)	1 oz
15 ml	vegetable oil	1 tbsp
15 g	butter	½ oz
60 ml	dry white wine	4 tbsp
375 g	French beans	12 oz
18-24	mussels	18-24
125 ml	chicken stock	4 fl oz
1	small bunch of fresh chives	1
	salt and pepper	

INGREDIENTS

chicken

mussels

seasoned flour

butter

French beans

chicken stock

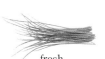

fresh chives

vegetable oil

white wine

ORDER OF WORK

1 SAUTE THE CHICKEN

2 COOK THE FRENCH BEANS

3 CLEAN THE MUSSELS

4 FINISH COOKING THE SAUTE

1 SAUTE THE CHICKEN

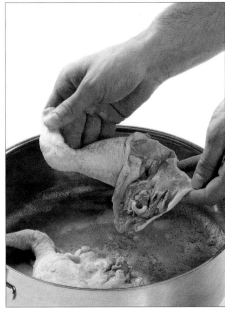

4 To test if the chicken is almost tender, pierce the meat with the 2-pronged fork: the chicken should fall easily from the fork. If some pieces cook before others, remove them and keep them warm.

1 Joint the chicken into 6 pieces (see steps 1-4 of How to Joint a Chicken into 8 Pieces, page 29). Put the seasoned flour in the shallow dish. Dip the chicken joints in the seasoned flour and pat off the excess with your hands to obtain an even coating.

2 Heat the oil and butter in the sauté pan over moderate heat until foaming. Add the chicken legs, skin side down, and sauté until they begin to brown, about 5 minutes. Add the breast pieces and continue cooking gently until very brown, about 10-15 minutes longer. Turn and brown the other side.

Low, straight sides allow steam to escape

3 Add the wine to the chicken. Cover and cook until the chicken is almost tender, 10-20 minutes. While the chicken is cooking, prepare the French beans and mussels (see page 58).

Wide heavy base of pan gives even heat

! TAKE CARE !
Use a long-handled, 2-pronged fork like this to protect your hands from intense heat and steam.

2 COOK THE FRENCH BEANS

1 With your fingers, snap the ends off the beans. Put the beans in the colander and rinse them under cold running water.

2 Bring a large saucepan of salted water to the boil. Add the beans and cook until just tender, 5-8 minutes for medium beans; tiny beans may take as little as 3-4 minutes, large beans up to 12 minutes.

3 Drain the beans in the colander, rinse them under cold running water to stop the cooking, then leave them to drain again thoroughly.

3 CLEAN THE MUSSELS

1 Scrub the mussels under cold running water with the stiff brush, discarding any with broken shells or that do not close when tapped. Using the small knife, scrape off any barnacles from the shells. Detach and discard any weeds or 'beards' from the mussels.

ANNE SAYS
'To clean barnacles quickly from mussels, rub 2 shells together.'

Mussel shells should be tightly closed

Detach stringy 'beards' – mussels use these to cling to poles or ropes where they grow

! TAKE CARE !
While cleaning mussels, discard any with cracked or broken shells or that do not close after washing. After cooking, discard any that have not opened.

4 FINISH COOKING THE SAUTE

1 Set the mussels on top of all the chicken pieces in the sauté pan, cover and cook until the mussels open, about 5 minutes.

2 With the slotted spoon and 2-pronged fork, transfer the mussels and chicken to a baking dish. Cover with foil and keep warm in a low oven. Add the chicken stock to the pan and boil until the sauce is reduced and slightly syrupy, 3-5 minutes, stirring occasionally.

Remove chicken and mussels from sauté pan while you finish sauce

3 Chop the chives. Return the chicken, mussels and French beans to the sauté pan with the chopped chives and heat gently 2-3 minutes. Taste for seasoning.

¶O¶ TO SERVE
Put the chicken pieces on individual plates with the mussels and beans. Spoon sauce over and around.

VARIATION

CHICKEN WITH CLAMS

In this variation, the chicken is combined with fresh clams, available from good fishmongers.

1 Replace the mussels with the same amount of clams, cleaning and cooking the clams in exactly the same way as the mussels.
2 For an attractive presentation, top each portion of chicken with 2-3 crossed chive stems.
3 Plainly cooked rice is a good accompaniment for this dish.

Steamed mussels are delicious with chicken

PINWHEEL CHICKEN WITH HERBS AND GOAT'S CHEESE

🍽 SERVES 4   🥄 WORK TIME 30-40 MINUTES   🍲 COOKING TIME 15-20 MINUTES

EQUIPMENT

medium bowl

chef's knife

boning knife

rolling pin

fork

metal spoon

large wide pan

slotted spoon

palette knife

kitchen scissors

whisk

small saucepan

chopping board

metal skewer

greaseproof paper

kitchen paper

aluminium foil

This dish uses flattened chicken breasts, rolled with a herb and goat's cheese stuffing, then poached. When sliced, the pretty green filling makes a spiral pattern, hence the name pinwheel. A simple, steamed vegetable, such as tiny courgettes, balances the tomato butter sauce.

GETTING AHEAD

The chicken rolls can be cooked, drained and kept in their foil in the refrigerator for up to 24 hours. Reheat them in a pan of simmering water for 7-10 minutes – be careful not to overcook them or they will be tough.

metric	SHOPPING LIST	imperial
4	large skinless, boneless chicken breasts, total weight about 750 g (1½ lb)	4
1	small bunch of fresh basil	1
1	small bunch of fresh parsley	1
3	sprigs of fresh thyme	3
125 g	goat's cheese	4 oz
30-45 ml	single cream, if necessary	2-3 tbsp
	juice of ½ lemon	
	salt and pepper	
	For the tomato butter sauce	
3	shallots	3
250 ml	dry white wine	8 fl oz
125 g	butter	4 oz
15 ml	tomato purée	1 tbsp

INGREDIENTS

goat's cheese

chicken breasts

fresh thyme

fresh basil

white wine

tomato purée

shallots

single cream

butter

fresh parsley

lemon juice

ORDER OF WORK

1 PREPARE THE CHICKEN BREASTS

2 STUFF THE BREASTS

3 COOK THE CHICKEN ROLLS

4 MAKE THE TOMATO BUTTER SAUCE

5 FINISH THE DISH

1 PREPARE THE CHICKEN BREASTS

1 Remove the tendon from each chicken breast: stroke out the tendon with the boning knife to remove it cleanly. Separate the fillet from the breast by lifting the end of the fillet and pulling it towards you. Set the fillets aside.

2 With the chef's knife, split the chicken breast open by slicing three-quarters of the way through the meat; hold it firmly with the flat of your hand, so the long straight edge of the breast forms the hinge. Open the split breast, like a book, and place it between 2 sheets of moistened greaseproof paper. Repeat for the remaining chicken breasts.

3 Pound the split-open breasts lightly with the rolling pin to obtain flat steaks of even thickness.

ANNE SAYS
'You can also use a meat mallet for flattening the chicken breasts.'

Cover with paper to prevent rolling pin from sticking

2 STUFF THE BREASTS

1 Chop the basil, parsley and thyme with the chef's knife.

2 Put the goat's cheese in the bowl and mash with the fork (harder cheese may be crumbled by hand), discarding any rind. If the cheese is too dry, soften it with the cream.

Add cream to cheese if it is dry

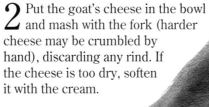

3 Add the herbs and lemon juice to the cheese and mix thoroughly. Taste for seasoning.

ANNE SAYS
'Fresh goat's cheese will be soft enough to mash without added liquid. More mature cheese will have a drier, more crumbly texture and will need cream to soften it so that it can be spread.'

4 Peel the top sheet of greaseproof paper from each breast. With the palette knife, evenly spread a quarter of the herb and goat's cheese filling in the centre of each breast.

Spread goat's cheese and herb filling in even layer over flattened chicken breast

Leave border of chicken breast clear all around so that filling will not be squeezed out when breast is rolled up

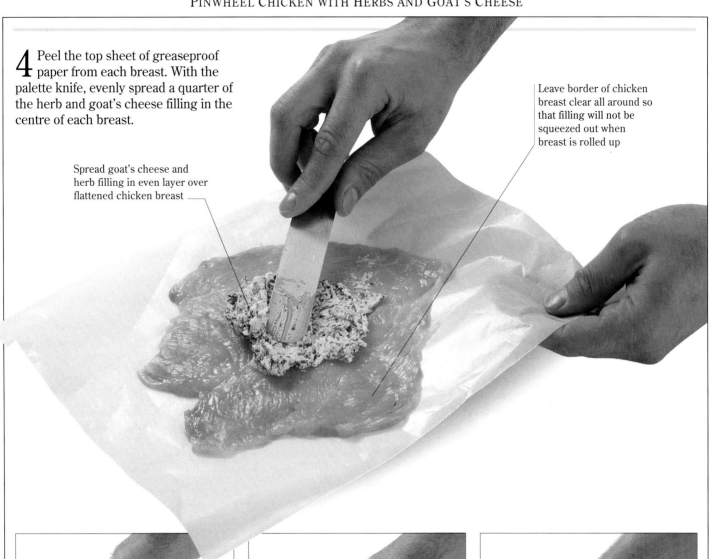

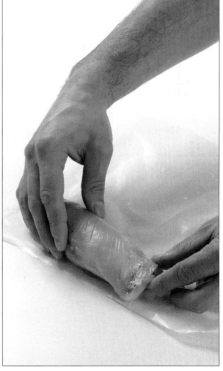

5 Put the fillet on top of the filling, along one long edge of a breast. Loosen the breast from the paper.

6 Roll the chicken breast up into a neat cylinder, beginning with the fillet-topped end.

7 Fold in the ends of the roll so the filling is sealed in securely. Repeat with the remaining breasts.

3 COOK THE CHICKEN ROLLS

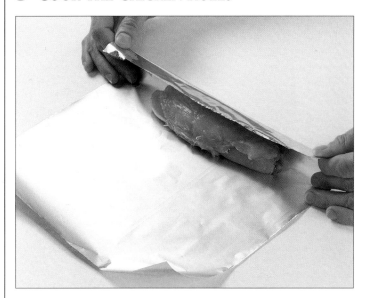

1 Cut a piece of foil to wrap generously around a rolled breast. Put it on the work surface, shiny-side down. Set the breast on the foil.

2 Roll up the stuffed breast in the foil neatly and tightly, smoothing the foil to keep it taut.

3 Twist the ends of the foil firmly to form a tight cylinder, sealing in the ends. Repeat the process for the remaining rolled breasts.

4 Half fill the wide pan with water and bring to the boil. With the slotted spoon, put the foil packages in the water and simmer until the skewer inserted in the centre of a package is hot to the touch when withdrawn, about 15 minutes. Keep the chicken rolls warm in their foil packages in the pan of hot (not boiling) water while you make the sauce.

Replace packages in hot water to keep warm

4 MAKE THE TOMATO BUTTER SAUCE

2 Off the heat, whisk in the butter, a few small pieces at a time, whisking constantly and moving the pan on and off the heat. Do not boil; the butter should thicken the sauce creamily without melting to oil.

1 Finely chop the shallots. In the small saucepan, boil the shallots and wine, with a small pinch each of salt and pepper until reduced to a syrupy glaze.

Add butter one piece at a time and wait until it melts and is absorbed before adding next

3 Whisk in the tomato purée and taste for seasoning.

! TAKE CARE !
Butter sauces are delicate, and separate easily if overheated. To keep them warm, set the saucepan in another pan of warm, not hot, water. Whisk occasionally but never leave for more than 30 minutes.

5 FINISH THE DISH

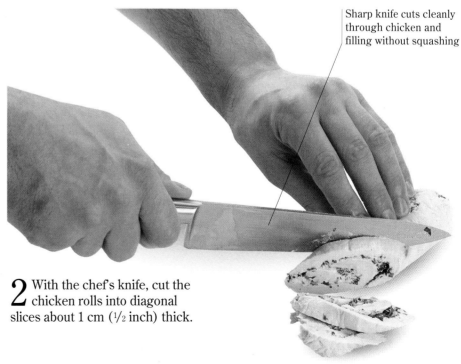

Sharp knife cuts cleanly through chicken and filling without squashing

1 Remove the chicken rolls from the pan with the slotted spoon and carefully unwrap them on kitchen paper to absorb any water.

2 With the chef's knife, cut the chicken rolls into diagonal slices about 1 cm (½ inch) thick.

PINWHEEL CHICKEN ITALIENNE

In this recipe, flattened chicken breasts are rolled with Parma ham and nutty-flavoured fontina cheese.

3 Spoon the sauce on to warmed individual plates, arrange the pinwheel slices on top and serve.

1 Prepare the chicken breasts as for Pinwheel Chicken with Herbs and Goat's Cheese.

2 Trim 4 large pieces, or 8 smaller pieces, of thinly sliced Parma ham the same size as the flattened breasts. Set the ham on the chicken.

3 Cut a 125 g (4 oz) piece of fontina cheese into thin slices, discarding the rind. Lay the cheese along one long side of each breast and put the fillet on top.

4 Roll up, wrap in foil and poach the breasts as directed.

5 Prepare the butter sauce, omitting the tomato purée.

6 For an attractive presentation, strain the sauce to separate the shallots, then garnish with the shallots and steamed finely diced courgettes.

Fan-cut courgette is simple to prepare but looks very elegant

Cherry tomatoes and mint sprig add colour to presentation

ORIENTAL STIR-FRIED CHICKEN

🍽 SERVES 4　🥣 WORK TIME 15-20 MINUTES*　🍲 COOKING TIME 10-12 MINUTES

EQUIPMENT

wok with wooden spatula**

baking sheet

chef's knife

boning knife

spoon

sieve　　kitchen paper

bowls

chopping board

**large heavy frying pan can also be used

ANNE SAYS
'*After cooking, do not wash your wok but wipe it out while still warm with a damp cloth or kitchen paper.*'

Stir-frying invites endless variations – the key is to use fresh ingredients, finely cut to ensure quick, even cooking. Here chicken is marinated and combined with Chinese mushrooms and almonds.

GETTING AHEAD
The vegetables and chicken can be prepared up to 1 hour ahead, and the almonds toasted a day in advance.

* plus 25-30 minutes marinating and soaking time

INGREDIENTS

chicken breasts

dried Chinese　　broccoli
black mushrooms

celery sticks　　onion

flaked　　vegetable　　sesame
almonds　　oil　　oil

rice wine　　soy sauce　　cornflour

metric	SHOPPING LIST	imperial
30 g	dried Chinese black mushrooms, or other dried wild mushrooms	1 oz
250 ml	warm water, more if needed	8 fl oz
45 g	flaked almonds	1½ oz
1	medium onion	1
4	celery sticks	4
500 g	head of broccoli	1 lb
2	skinless, boneless chicken breasts, total weight about 375 g (12 oz)	2
90 ml	vegetable oil	3 fl oz
5 ml	sesame oil	1 tsp
	For the marinade	
60 ml	soy sauce	4 tbsp
60 ml	rice wine or dry sherry	4 tbsp
10 ml	cornflour	2 tsp

ORDER OF WORK

1　PREPARE THE VEGETABLES AND ALMONDS

2　SLICE AND MARINATE THE CHICKEN

3　COOK THE STIR-FRY

1 PREPARE THE VEGETABLES AND ALMONDS

1 Put the mushrooms in a bowl, cover with the warm water and allow to soften 30 minutes.

ANNE SAYS

'If you cannot find dried Chinese or wild mushrooms, use 250 g (8 oz) fresh mushrooms, cleaned and sliced, instead.'

2 Meanwhile, toast the almonds and prepare the remaining vegetables. Heat the oven to 190°C (375°F, Gas 5). Spread the almonds evenly on the baking sheet and toast in the oven until lightly browned, 6-8 minutes.

3 Cut the onion in half lengthwise. Cut each half into 4-5 wedges.

4 Trim the ends from the celery sticks and cut the sticks crosswise, on the bias, into slices about 1 cm (½ inch) thick.

5 Cut off the broccoli heads, discarding the stalks. Cut the heads into very small florets.

6 Drain the mushrooms, reserving the liquid. Trim off any hard woody stalks, then slice the mushrooms. Strain the liquid through the sieve lined with kitchen paper to remove any grit or sand.

2 SLICE AND MARINATE THE CHICKEN

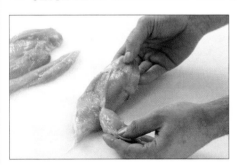

1 Remove the tendon from each chicken breast. Separate the fillet from each breast by lifting the end of the fillet and pulling it towards you. With the chef's knife, cut the fillet into thin strips.

2 Holding your hand firmly on top of the breast, cut the meat on the bias into very thin slices. You should get 10-15 slices from each breast.

3 In a bowl, mix together the soy sauce, rice wine and cornflour, stirring until the cornflour is dissolved. Add the chicken and stir until coated. Marinate about 15 minutes while you cook the vegetables.

Stir chicken to mix with marinade

3 COOK THE STIR-FRY

1 Heat half of the vegetable oil in the wok. Add the onion and celery and stir and toss over quite high heat until the vegetables are beginning to soften, 1-2 minutes.

2 Add the broccoli and fry, stirring and tossing constantly, until beginning to soften, 2-3 minutes. Stir the mushrooms into the vegetables and cook, stirring and tossing, 2 minutes.

3 Remove all the vegetables from the wok to a bowl and set aside in a warm place.

4 Wipe the wok with kitchen paper. Add the remaining vegetable oil to the wok and heat it.

! TAKE CARE !
If using fresh mushrooms, be sure to cook them until all liquid has evaporated.

Tip warm vegetables back into wok

5 Drain the chicken slices and strips, reserving the marinade liquid. Add the chicken to the wok and cook over high heat, stirring and tossing, until the chicken is no longer opaque, 2-3 minutes.

6 Return the vegetables to the wok and stir to mix with the chicken. Add 60 ml (4 tbsp) of the reserved, strained mushroom soaking liquid.

7 Pour in the reserved marinade liquid and cook, stirring, 2 minutes. As the marinade liquid cooks, the cornflour will slightly thicken the sauce. Sprinkle the stir-fry with the sesame oil, stir and taste for seasoning, adding more soy sauce, rice wine or sesame oil to your taste.

8 Sprinkle the toasted almonds over the stir-fry and serve in individual bowls.

Chicken slices are delicately flavoured with rice wine and soy sauce

V A R I A T I O N

SWEET AND SOUR STIR-FRIED CHICKEN

Here pineapple replaces the broccoli and mushrooms and pineapple juice gives sweetness to the sauce.

1 Prepare the chicken breasts as directed in the main recipe.
2 For the marinade, reduce the rice wine to 15 ml (1 tbsp); add 15 ml (1 tbsp) wine vinegar and 15 ml (1 tbsp) caster sugar.
3 Omit the broccoli and mushrooms and replace with 4 rings of canned pineapple cut into small pieces.
4 Finish as directed, adding 60 ml (4 tbsp) pineapple juice from the can instead of the mushroom soaking liquid.

Chopsticks are the ideal eating utensils

YORKSHIRE CHICKEN WITH STUFFED PRUNES

Hindle Wakes

🍴 SERVES 4 🥣 WORK TIME 30 MINUTES* 🍲 COOKING TIME 1¼-1½ HOURS

EQUIPMENT

 chef's knife

shallow dishes

food processor

chopping board

trussing needle and string

2-pronged fork

wooden spoon

grater

medium baking dish

saucepans

large metal spoon

lemon squeezer

whisk

kitchen string

bowls

large flameproof casserole or pot with lid

sieve

Tradition has it that Hindle Wakes was created to reward those who kept watch or 'wake' on the eve of a great festival.

* *plus 1 hour soaking time*

metric	SHOPPING LIST	imperial
1.8 kg	boiling fowl, with liver	4 lb
2	medium carrots	2
1	bouquet garni (see box, page 72)	1
2	cloves	2
1	medium onion	1
2	garlic cloves	2
5 ml	black peppercorns	1 tsp
300 ml	medium dry white wine	½ pint
1.5 litres	chicken stock or water	2 ⅓ pints
	salt and pepper	
	For the stuffing	
250 g	large stoneless prunes	8 oz
1	small onion	1
125 g	butter + extra for baking dish	4 oz
1	bunch of fresh parsley	1
1	lemon	1
10	slices of white bread, total weight about 250 g (8 oz)	10
125 ml	chicken stock	4 fl oz
	For the velouté sauce	
75 g	butter	2 ½ oz
45 g	flour	1 ½ oz
175 ml	double cream	6 fl oz
	lemon juice	

INGREDIENTS

garlic cloves

boiling fowl

onion

prunes

lemon

fresh parsley

slices of white bread

carrots

cloves

black peppercorns

double cream

chicken stock

bouquet garni

butter

white wine

flour

ORDER OF WORK

1 PREPARE THE STUFFING

2 TRUSS AND POACH THE CHICKEN

3 COOK THE PRUNES AND STUFFING

4 MAKE THE VELOUTE SAUCE

1 PREPARE THE STUFFING

1 Put the prunes in a bowl and cover with hot water. Allow to soak until softened and plump, about 1 hour, then drain. Set aside 8-12 of the firmest prunes to be stuffed; chop the rest.

Reserve firmest, whole prunes for stuffing

Chop remaining prunes coarsely

2 Finely chop the onion. Heat half of the butter in a small saucepan, add the onion and fry until soft but not brown, 2-3 minutes.

3 Cut any membrane from the chicken liver, then chop it.

4 Stir the chicken liver into the onion and cook until brown, 1-2 minutes. Turn into a bowl.

5 With the chef's knife, finely chop the parsley.

6 Grate the zest from the lemon, then cut the lemon in half and squeeze the juice.

! TAKE CARE !
When grating lemon, be careful not to catch the white pith because it is bitter.

Use squeezer that will catch lemon pips

7 Break up the bread and work it in the food processor to make crumbs. Melt the remaining butter in a small saucepan.

8 Add the chopped prunes, breadcrumbs, parsley and lemon zest to the bowl. Stir in the chicken stock, lemon juice and melted butter. Season well to taste with salt and pepper. Set aside.

Stir stuffing ingredients to combine thoroughly

HOW TO MAKE A BOUQUET GARNI

This bundle of aromatic flavouring herbs is designed to be easily lifted from the pot and discarded at the end of cooking. To make, hold 2-3 sprigs of thyme, 1 bay leaf and 10-12 parsley stalks together. Wind a piece of string around the herbs and tie securely, leaving a length of string to tie to pot handle.

2 TRUSS AND POACH THE CHICKEN

1 Truss the chicken. Put the chicken into the casserole (it should just fit). Cut the carrots into quarters and add to the casserole. Add the bouquet garni, tying the string to the handle so that it can be removed easily at the end of cooking.

2 Stick the cloves into the onion and add to the casserole with the garlic and peppercorns.

4 Bring to the boil, skimming well, then cover and simmer over low heat, skimming occasionally, 1¼ - 1½ hours.

3 Add the white wine with enough chicken stock or water to cover the chicken above the legs. Season lightly with salt.

Skim off froth and impurities from time to time during simmering

5 Halfway through cooking, turn the chicken over so that it cooks evenly. (At this point, cook the prunes and stuffing, see page 74.) The chicken is done when the thigh meat is tender and no pink juice runs out when it is pierced with the 2-pronged fork.

Use 2-pronged fork and spoon or ladle to turn chicken over gently so that cooking liquid does not splash out of casserole

6 When the chicken is cooked, remove it from the casserole, wrap it in foil, and keep warm; reserve the cooking liquid for the sauce.

3 COOK THE PRUNES AND STUFFING

Add about
1 teaspoonful
of filling

1 Heat the oven to 190°C (375°F, Gas 5). Fill the whole prunes with stuffing. Butter the baking dish. Spread the remaining stuffing in it.

2 Arrange the stuffed prunes on top of the stuffing and cover the dish with foil. Bake until very hot, 30-40 minutes. Take out and keep warm.

4 MAKE THE VELOUTE SAUCE

Pour liquid
through sieve
set in bowl

1 Skim any fat from the cooking liquid and discard. Boil the cooking liquid until reduced by half.

2 Strain the cooking liquid and measure it: there should be about 750 ml (1¼ pints). Add more stock or water if necessary. Discard the vegetables and bouquet garni.

3 Melt the butter in a medium saucepan. Whisk in the flour.

4 Cook the mixture until foaming but not browned, 1-2 minutes, whisking well.

5 Add the cooking liquid and heat, whisking constantly, until the sauce comes to the boil and thickens. Add the cream and simmer 2 minutes. Take from the heat, stir in lemon juice and seasoning to taste, and keep warm.

🍽 **TO SERVE** Cut the stuffing into wedges. Remove the trussing strings from the chicken, carve it, arrange on plates and coat with sauce. Place the prunes and stuffing next to the chicken. Serve the rest of the sauce separately.

Whisk constantly as you add strained liquid

—— **GETTING AHEAD** ——
Chicken, prunes and stuffing can be prepared a day ahead. Refrigerate chicken in cooking liquid; reheat and make the sauce just before serving.

Baked stuffing is cut into attractive wedges for serving

Carrots, here cut into fine julienne, make a delightful colour contrast on plate

CHICKEN IN PARSLEY SAUCE

1 Remove the stalks from a bunch of parsley and lightly crush them with a rolling pin to release all the flavour; chop the sprigs.
2 Poach the chicken as directed in the main recipe, adding the parsley stalks to the cooking liquid.
3 Omit the stuffing and prunes.
4 Prepare the sauce as directed and add the chopped parsley with the lemon juice.

ANNE SAYS
'*To preserve the bright green colour of chopped parsley, blanch it before adding it to the sauce: sprinkle the parsley into a small saucepan of boiling water, simmer 5 seconds and drain in a fine sieve. Rinse the parsley under cold water and spread out to dry on kitchen paper.*'

AMERICAN BRUNSWICK STEW

 SERVES 4-6   WORK TIME 25-35 MINUTES COOKING TIME 2-2½ HOURS

EQUIPMENT

large flameproof casserole with lid

sieve

small knife

chef's knife

large metal spoon

2-pronged fork

slotted spoon

bowls

chopping board

forks

wooden spoon

saucepans, 1 with lid

kitchen string

shallow dish

ANNE SAYS
'If you don't have a bacon hock, use a piece of smoked collar. Before serving the stew, cut the meat into dice, discarding any rind.'

Brunswick County in North Carolina and the county of the same name in Virginia both take credit for this famous colonial American stew. Two things are certain: the recipe uses Southern ingredients – smoked bacon, beans, sweetcorn and hot pepper – and was originally made with squirrel and without vegetables!

GETTING AHEAD
The stew can be cooked 2 days ahead and kept refrigerated; in fact, the flavour mellows on standing. This stew also freezes well for up to 3 months.

metric	SHOPPING LIST	imperial
1.5 kg	chicken	3½ lb
500 g	smoked bacon hock	1 lb
1.5 litres	water, more if needed	2⅓ pints
15 ml	dark soft brown sugar	1 tbsp
1	bouquet garni	1
1	medium onion	1
3	celery sticks	3
375 g	tomatoes	12 oz
250 g	shelled fresh or thawed frozen broad beans	8 oz
210 g	fresh or thawed frozen sweetcorn	7 oz
375 g	potatoes	12 oz
5 ml	dried hot red pepper flakes	1 tsp
	salt and pepper	

INGREDIENTS

chicken

onion

smoked bacon hock

sweetcorn

tomatoes

bouquet garni

potatoes

dark soft brown sugar

broad beans

dried hot red pepper flakes

celery sticks

ORDER OF WORK

COOK THE CHICKEN

2 PREPARE AND COOK THE VEGETABLES

3 COOK THE POTATOES AND FINISH THE STEW

1 COOK THE CHICKEN

1 Joint the chicken into 6 pieces (see steps 1-4, How to Joint a Chicken into 8 Pieces, page 29). Put the chicken joints in the casserole with the bacon hock and pour in enough water to cover. Add the sugar and bouquet garni. Bring to the boil and skim well with the slotted spoon.

2 Cover and simmer gently until the chicken joints are almost tender when pierced with the 2-pronged fork, about 1 hour.

3 Lift out the chicken with the slotted spoon and reserve it. Remove the casserole from the heat and set aside.

HOW TO SKIN, SEED AND CHOP TOMATOES

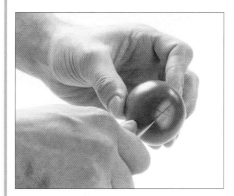

1 With a small knife, cut the core out of each tomato, then turn the tomato over and mark a cross on the base. Immerse the tomatoes in a pan of boiling water 8-15 seconds, depending on ripeness, until the skin curls away from the cross.

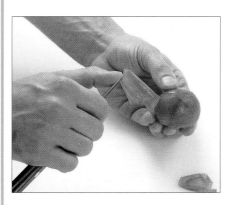

3 When the tomatoes are cool, drain them and peel away the skin, using the small knife.

5 Set each tomato half cut side down on a chopping board and slice it with a chef's knife. Turn the slices through 90° and slice them again.

2 With a slotted spoon, lift the tomatoes out of the water and transfer them to a bowl of cold water.

Squeeze out seeds into sieve so that juices can be reserved

4 Halve each tomato crosswise like a grapefruit. Squeeze each half firmly in your fist to remove the seeds, scraping off remaining seeds with the knife.

6 Coarsely chop the tomatoes into rough dice.

2 PREPARE AND COOK THE VEGETABLES

Drain thawed frozen corn before adding

1 Chop the onion. Trim and thinly slice the celery. Skin, seed and coarsely chop the tomatoes (see box, page 77).

2 Bring the chicken liquid in the casserole back to the boil. Add the onion, celery, tomatoes and beans to the chicken liquid and simmer, stirring often, until the beans are nearly tender, 20-30 minutes.

3 Add the sweetcorn and simmer 10 minutes longer. While the vegetables are simmering, cook the potatoes (see below).

3 COOK THE POTATOES AND FINISH THE STEW

1 Cut the potatoes into equal chunks and put them in a saucepan of salted water. Bring to the boil, then cover and simmer them until tender when pierced with the point of the small knife, 15-20 minutes. Drain the potatoes in the sieve, then work them through the sieve with the wooden spoon.

ANNE SAYS
'*You can crush the potatoes with a potato masher if you prefer. Just drain off the water using the saucepan lid and crush the potatoes in the saucepan.*'

Press potatoes through sieve to purée finely

2 Stir the potatoes and red pepper flakes into the stew and season to taste. Return the chicken joints to the stew and simmer, stirring often, until the chicken is very tender, about 15 minutes longer.

ANNE SAYS
'*You can also use a food mill for puréeing the potatoes.*'

! TAKE CARE !
Do not use a food processor or electric mixer because this will give the potatoes a gluey consistency.

3 Lift out the bacon. Using a fork and knife, pull the meat from the bones, discarding the skin and fat.

4 Shred the meat with 2 forks and stir it back into the stew. The sauce should be thick, but if it is sticky, add a little more water. Discard the bouquet garni and taste for seasoning.

⏀ TO SERVE

Serve the stew from the casserole or in individual bowls.

V A R I A T I O N

CHICKEN STEW BASQUAISE

1 Double the amount of tomatoes in the main recipe, and omit the brown sugar, beans and sweetcorn.
2 Roast, peel and core 2 red peppers and 2 green peppers and cut them into strips.
3 Add the peppers to the stew with the tomatoes.

V A R I A T I O N

CHICKEN WITH KIDNEY BEANS AND GARLIC SAUSAGE

Replacing the broad beans and sweetcorn with red kidney beans and garlic sausage gives colour and spice to this variation of Brunswick Stew.

1 Soak 500 g (1 lb) dried red kidney beans in cold water to cover by 10 cm (4 inches) 6-8 hours; drain.
2 Put the beans in a pot and add 1 onion stuck with a clove and a bouquet garni. Cover generously with water and bring to the boil. Boil at least 5 minutes, then simmer 25 minutes; add salt and simmer about 45 minutes longer.
3 Drain the beans, discarding the onion and bouquet garni.
4 Thickly slice a 375 g (12 oz) piece of garlic sausage, discarding the skin.
5 Prepare and cook the chicken as directed in the main recipe. Omit the broad beans and sweetcorn. Add the kidney beans with the onion, tomatoes and celery and simmer until the beans are nearly tender, about 30 minutes.
6 Thicken the stew with the potatoes, and add the sausage when you return the chicken to the stew.

Chicken and vegetables are a meal in themselves, needing only crusty bread as an accompaniment

CHICKEN IN A PAPER CASE WITH JULIENNE VEGETABLES

Suprêmes de Poulet en Papillote à la Julienne

🍽 SERVES 4 🥣 WORK TIME 30-40 MINUTES 🍲 COOKING TIME 10-15 MINUTES

EQUIPMENT

shallow dishes

kitchen scissors

large sauté pan with lid

pastry brush

pencil

boning knife

chef's knife

2-pronged fork

wooden spoon

baking parchment

metal spoon

fork

baking sheet(s)

chopping board

small bowl

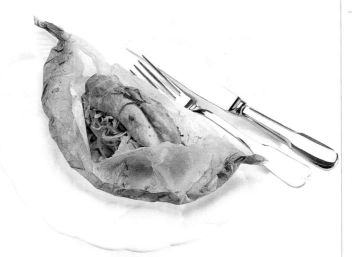

These puffed, golden-brown paper cases should be broken open at the table, so the aromas of the chicken, herbs and vegetables can be fully appreciated by each diner. Take advantage of the seasons, altering the vegetables and herbs to follow your inspiration – tender asparagus spears with chives or chervil in the spring, wild mushrooms with rosemary in the autumn.

GETTING AHEAD

The chicken breasts can be prepared and sealed in their paper cases up to 2 hours ahead and refrigerated. Bake them just before serving.

metric	SHOPPING LIST	imperial
4	skinless, boneless chicken breasts, total weight 750 g (1½ lb)	4
30 g	seasoned flour	1 oz
15 ml	vegetable oil	1 tbsp
90 g	butter	3 oz
1	bunch of fresh tarragon	1
2	medium carrots	2
3	celery sticks	3
1	medium turnip	1
	salt and pepper	
1	egg for glaze	1

INGREDIENTS

chicken breasts

egg

seasoned flour

vegetable oil

turnip

butter

fresh tarragon

celery sticks

carrots

ORDER OF WORK

1 **PREPARE THE CHICKEN BREASTS**

2 **PREPARE THE VEGETABLES**

3 **COOK THE VEGETABLES**

4 **MAKE THE PAPER CASES AND BAKE**

1 PREPARE THE CHICKEN BREASTS

1 With the boning knife, gently stroke the tendon from each chicken breast to remove it cleanly.

Chicken breasts should have even coating of seasoned flour

2 Separate the fillet from each breast by lifting an end of the fillet and pulling it towards you. With the chef's knife, cut the fillet into thin strips on the diagonal.

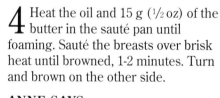

3 Put the seasoned flour in a dish. Dip the chicken breasts in the flour; pat off the excess for an even coating.

4 Heat the oil and 15 g (½ oz) of the butter in the sauté pan until foaming. Sauté the breasts over brisk heat until browned, 1-2 minutes. Turn and brown on the other side.

ANNE SAYS
'*If the pan is small, sauté the chicken breasts in 2 batches.*'

5 Transfer the breasts to a shallow dish and allow to cool. (The meat will not be cooked through at this point; cooking is finished in the oven.)

6 Add the strips of fillet meat to the pan and sauté over moderate heat, stirring, until they are no longer opaque, about 1 minute. Remove and allow to cool. Wipe the sauté pan.

7 When the breasts are cool enough to handle, cut a pocket in each, holding them flat with your hand.

2 PREPARE THE VEGETABLES

1 Reserve 4 sprigs of tarragon for garnish. Remove the leaves from the remaining tarragon sprigs and chop them.

Julienne vegetables cook quickly and look very decorative

Cut vegetables into fine matchstick-sized strips

2 With the chef's knife, cut the carrots, celery sticks and turnip into julienne strips (see box, right).

HOW TO CUT JULIENNE VEGETABLES

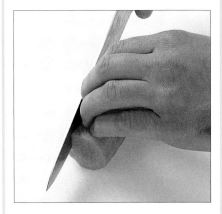

1 For round vegetables such as carrots, cut a thin strip from one side so that the vegetable will lie flat on the board.

2 Cut the vegetable crosswise into 5 cm (2 inch) lengths, then lengthwise into thin vertical slices.

3 Stack the slices, 6 or so at a time, and cut lengthwise into very fine strips, guiding the knife with your curled fingers. Use a strip as a guide for length when cutting other vegetables.

3 COOK THE VEGETABLES

1 First make a paper lid to fit the sauté pan: fold a square of baking parchment in half and then in half again to make a triangle.

2 Fold the triangle of baking parchment over once or twice more to form a slender cone.

4 Warm 60 g (2 oz) of the remaining butter until soft and brush a little over the paper round. Heat the remaining butter in the sauté pan. Add the vegetable julienne with salt and pepper to taste.

Position tip of cone over centre of pan

Cut to size so paper will fit neatly inside pan

3 Holding the paper cone over the pan with the tip at the centre, use the edge of the pan as a gauge to cut the cone. Unfold the paper round.

Cover vegetables with buttered paper and then with lid so they cook gently in their own juices

5 Set the paper round on the vegetables, butter side down. Cover the pan with the lid and cook over low heat, stirring occasionally, until the vegetables are tender, 15-20 minutes.

! TAKE CARE !
Do not let the vegetables brown.

4 MAKE THE PAPER CASES AND BAKE

1 Take a sheet of baking parchment measuring 38 x 45 cm (15 x 18 inches) and fold it in half. Put one chicken breast on the paper and draw a curve to make a heart shape when unfolded. It should be at least 7.5 cm (3 inches) larger all around. Cut along the curve to make a heart shape, cutting inside the drawn line. Repeat to make a total of 4 paper hearts.

Draw heart shape on folded paper

ANNE SAYS
'*Foil is a practical alternative to baking parchment for the parcels, but the presentation is less impressive because foil does not puff and brown.*'

2 Open out the paper hearts and brush each one with softened butter, leaving a border of about 2.5 cm (1 inch) unbuttered.

3 For the glaze, use the fork to beat the egg with a pinch of salt. Brush the egg glaze on the unbuttered border of each paper heart.

4 Heat the oven to 180°C (350°F, Gas 4). Stir the strips of chicken fillet into the vegetables and add the chopped tarragon. Mix well and taste for seasoning.

5 Spoon a bed of the julienne filling on one half of a paper heart. Spoon more filling into the pocket of one of the chicken breasts and set it on the bed of vegetables. Lay a sprig of tarragon on top of the breast.

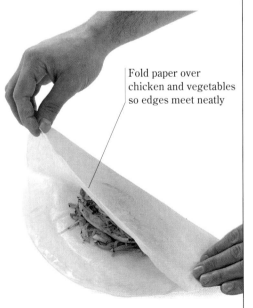

Fold paper over chicken and vegetables so edges meet neatly

6 Fold the paper over the breast and run your finger along the edge to stick the 2 sides of the paper heart together.

CHICKEN IN A PAPER CASE WITH PEPPERS
Suprêmes de Poulet en Papillote Basquaise

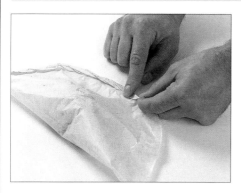

7 Make small pleats to seal the edges of the paper case.

8 Twist the 'tails' of the paper case to finish. Repeat the process with the remaining ingredients to make 4 paper parcels.

9 Lay the paper cases on the baking sheet(s) and bake them in the heated oven until puffed and brown, 10-12 minutes.

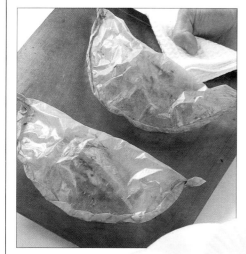

🍴 TO SERVE
At once, transfer the puffed, brown parcels to warmed individual plates and serve, Each person can open his or her own chicken-filled paper case.

1 Replace the carrots, celery and turnip with 1 green pepper, 1 red pepper and 1 yellow pepper.
2 Core and seed the peppers, then cut them into thin strips. Cook them as for the carrots, celery and turnip.
3 Prepare the chicken breasts, fill the paper cases (omitting the tarragon) and bake as directed.

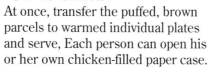

Chicken is moist and tender cooked this way

ANNE SAYS
'*If the parcels cool and deflate, they can be puffed again by warming briefly in the oven.*'

CHICKEN WITH CURRY DRESSING AND SAFFRON RICE

Salade de Poulet Indienne

 SERVES 4-6 WORK TIME 25-35 MINUTES COOKING TIME 20-30 MINUTES

EQUIPMENT

food processor*   sieve

small knife

chef's knife

rubber spatula

saucepans, 1 with lid

wooden spoon

forks

metal spoons

bowls

chopping board

shallow dish

whisk

*blender can also be used

The dressing used here is unusual, lightly thickened with cottage cheese and flavoured with curry and chutney. Saffron rice provides a brilliant background to the cold roast chicken.

GETTING AHEAD

The curry dressing, saffron rice, tomatoes and vinaigrette dressing can be prepared up to 24 hours ahead.

metric	SHOPPING LIST	imperial
1.8 kg	whole cooked chicken	4 lb
45 ml	lemon juice	3 tbsp
175 ml	vegetable oil	6 fl oz
500 g	cherry tomatoes	1 lb
2.5 ml	paprika for sprinkling	½ tsp
For the saffron rice salad		
	saffron	
600 ml	water	1 pint
300 g	long-grain rice	10 oz
3	celery sticks	3
For the curry dressing		
1	small onion	1
90 ml	vegetable oil	3 fl oz
15 ml	curry powder	1 tbsp
60 ml	tomato juice	4 tbsp
60 ml	red wine vinegar	4 tbsp
10 ml	apricot jam	2 tsp
30 ml	lemon juice	2 tbsp
250 g	cottage cheese	8 oz
	salt and pepper	

INGREDIENTS

cherry tomatoes   onion

whole cooked chicken

apricot jam

saffron

lemon juice

cottage cheese

celery sticks

tomato juice

paprika

long-grain rice

curry powder

vegetable oil   red wine vinegar

ORDER OF WORK

1 MAKE THE SAFFRON RICE

2 MAKE THE CURRY DRESSING

3 PREPARE THE CHICKEN

4 FINISH THE RICE AND PREPARE THE CHERRY TOMATOES

1 MAKE THE SAFFRON RICE

1 Put a large pinch of saffron and a pinch of salt in a large saucepan with the water. Bring to the boil and simmer 2 minutes. Stir the rice into the saffron water and bring back to the boil. Cover and simmer until the rice is tender, 15-20 minutes. Let the rice cool 5-10 minutes, then stir with a fork and taste for seasoning. Set aside.

! TAKE CARE !
Do not stir the rice while it is very hot or the grains will break up.

Only a little saffron is needed to flavour and colour rice

2 MAKE THE CURRY DRESSING

1 Finely chop the onion. Heat 15 ml (1 tbsp) oil in a small saucepan over moderate heat. Add the chopped onion and sauté until soft but not brown, about 2 minutes, stirring occasionally.

2 Add the curry powder and cook gently 2 minutes, stirring. Add the tomato juice and vinegar and simmer until reduced by half.

! TAKE CARE !
Use a metal spoon for stirring the mixture because a wooden spoon will absorb strong flavours.

Pour oil in slowly, with machine running, so it is absorbed and dressing is emulsified

3 Stir in the apricot jam. Let the mixture cool, then transfer to the food processor or blender.

4 Blend until the mixture is smooth, scraping the bowl with the spatula as necessary.

5 Add the lemon juice and cottage cheese and blend until smooth. With the blades turning, pour in the remaining oil. Taste for seasoning.

3 PREPARE THE CHICKEN

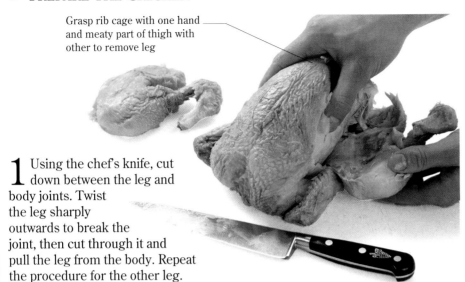

Grasp rib cage with one hand and meaty part of thigh with other to remove leg

1 Using the chef's knife, cut down between the leg and body joints. Twist the leg sharply outwards to break the joint, then cut through it and pull the leg from the body. Repeat the procedure for the other leg.

2 Slit along one side of the chicken breastbone. Using your fingers and the point of the knife, loosen the breast meat from the carcass and remove one side of the breast in one piece. Repeat on the other side.

4 Pull off the skin from the chicken breasts and discard it. Pull the meat into shreds with your fingers and pile on the dish.

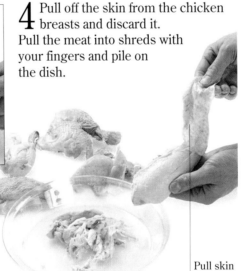

3 With your fingers, pull away the wishbone and the meat adhering to it. Pull off any remaining meat from the chicken carcass.

Pull skin up and off

5 Using your fingers and the point of the knife, tear and cut the meat from the leg bones. Trim away the tendons and discard the skin. Shred the meat with your fingers and add to the plate.

ANNE SAYS
'There should be about 500 g (1 lb) meat.'

4 FINISH THE RICE AND PREPARE THE CHERRY TOMATOES

1 Trim and thinly slice the celery. Stir gently into the cooled saffron rice with a fork. Transfer the mixture to a bowl.

2 Make a vinaigrette dressing: put the lemon juice, salt and pepper in a small bowl and whisk to combine. Add the oil in a thin stream, whisking constantly so that the dressing thickens slightly. Pour three-quarters of the dressing on to the rice and toss gently with 2 forks to combine. Reserve the remaining dressing.

ANNE SAYS
'Vinaigrette dressing can be kept for a week or more, in a tightly closed jar or bottle. It will separate, but a brisk shake will re-emulsify it.'

3 Put the tomatoes, in 2 batches, in the sieve and immerse them in a medium saucepan of boiling water 8-10 seconds. Drain the tomatoes and peel off the skin with the small knife. Mix them with the reserved vinaigrette dressing.

Tomatoes are easy to skin after blanching in boiling water

VARIATION

CHICKEN WITH TARRAGON DRESSING AND RICE

Chicken and tarragon are a natural pair.

1 Prepare the chicken and the cherry tomatoes as in the main recipe, cutting the chicken into slices.
2 Prepare the rice salad as directed but omit the saffron.
3 Replace the curry dressing with this dressing: purée 250 g (8 oz) cottage cheese in a food processor or blender with 15 ml (1 tbsp) tarragon vinegar. Chop 1 bunch of fresh tarragon and stir it into the puréed cottage cheese. Season to taste with salt and pepper.
4 Arrange on individual plates and garnish with a few sprigs of fresh tarragon.

🍽 TO SERVE

Toss the shredded chicken with half of the curry dressing. Pile the saffron rice salad in the centre of a platter and arrange the chicken on top. Sprinkle with paprika and garnish with the cherry tomatoes. Serve the remaining dressing separately.

Dressing for chicken is smooth and spicy

SOUTHERN FRIED CHICKEN WITH PAN GRAVY

  SERVES 4 WORK TIME 10-15 MINUTES* COOKING TIME 20-30 MINUTES

EQUIPMENT

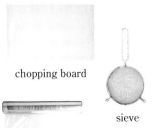
chopping board

sieve

cling film

shallow dishes

large bowl

whisk

chef's knife

plate

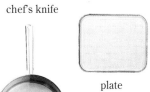

kitchen paper

large heavy frying pan

slotted spoon

large metal spoon

2-pronged fork

deep-fat thermometer

INGREDIENTS

chicken

milk

vegetable oil

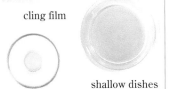
flour

This is an American favourite from the South. In this version, the chicken is soaked in milk to whiten the meat. The traditional accompaniment is mashed potatoes, accented if you like by a sprinkling of chopped fresh herbs like parsley or chives. Fried chicken, without the gravy, is also delicious served cold on a picnic, with a potato salad and some crisp vegetable sticks.

GETTING AHEAD
The chicken can soak up to 24 hours. If serving hot, do not fry in advance or the coating will be soggy.

* plus 8-12 hours soaking time

metric	SHOPPING LIST	imperial
1.5 kg	chicken	3 ½ lb
500 ml	milk, more if needed	16 fl oz
250 ml	vegetable oil for frying, more if needed	8 fl oz
60 g	seasoned flour made with 10 ml (2 tsp) pepper	2 oz
	For the gravy	
30 ml	flour	2 tbsp
375 ml	milk	12 fl oz
	salt and pepper	

ORDER OF WORK

1 PREPARE THE CHICKEN

2 MAKE THE GRAVY

1 PREPARE THE CHICKEN

Cube of bread will sizzle when oil is sufficiently hot

1 Joint the chicken into 8 pieces (see box, page 29). Put the chicken joints in a bowl and add enough milk to cover. Cover securely with cling film and soak for 8-12 hours.

3 Pour vegetable oil into the frying pan to make a 2 cm (¾ inch) deep layer. Heat the oil over moderate heat to 180°C (350°F) on the deep-fat thermometer.

ANNE SAYS
'*If you don't have a deep-fat thermometer, test the temperature of the oil by dropping a cube of fresh bread into it: if the bread turns golden brown in 1 minute, the oil is at about 180°C (350°F).*'

Flour chicken joints lightly

2 With the slotted spoon, transfer the chicken joints to a dish. Discard the milk.

4 Put the seasoned flour in the shallow dish. Dip the chicken joints in the flour and pat off the excess with your hands to obtain an even coating.

ANNE SAYS
'*To coat the chicken quickly, drop the joints into a plastic bag, add the seasoned flour, twist the bag closed and shake about 30 seconds.*'

5 Gently add the chicken joints to the pan, skin side down, taking care as the chicken may sputter. Fry until brown, 3-5 minutes.

6 Turn the chicken joints over and reduce the heat to low.

7 Continue frying until the chicken is brown and tender when pierced with the 2-pronged fork, 20-25 minutes. If some pieces cook before others, remove them and keep warm.

8 Transfer the chicken to a dish lined with kitchen paper and keep warm.

! TAKE CARE !
If keeping the chicken warm in a low oven, do not cover it or the crisp coating will soften.

Kitchen paper will absorb any oil that drains from chicken

Long prongs of fork protect fingers from spatters

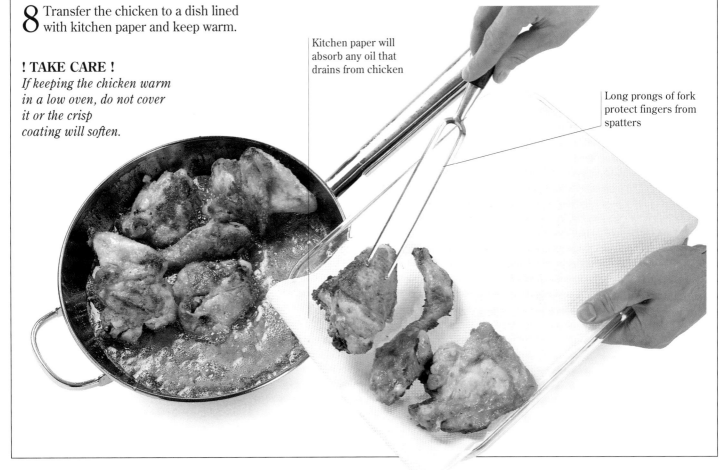

2 MAKE THE GRAVY

1 Discard all but about 30 ml (2 tbsp) of the fat from the frying pan. Sprinkle in the flour.

2 Cook, stirring with the large metal spoon, until browned, 2-3 minutes.

3 Whisk in the milk and simmer until thickened, about 2 minutes. Season the gravy to taste and strain into a gravy boat.

🍴 TO SERVE
Arrange the chicken pieces on a serving dish or individual plates. Serve the gravy separately.

Fried chicken joints are delicious hot or cold

V A R I A T I O N

BACON-FRIED CHICKEN

In this recipe, the chicken does not cook in as deep a layer of fat as in the Southern Fried Chicken, but the flavour of the bacon is wonderful and the gravy is spiked with a little Tabasco.

1 Soak the chicken in milk as in the main recipe.
2 Omit the vegetable oil for frying and sauté 8-12 bacon rashers until crisp and brown and all the fat is released. Remove the bacon, drain on kitchen paper and keep warm.
3 Flour the chicken as directed, then cook in the bacon fat and drain on kitchen paper.
4 Prepare the pan gravy, adding a dash of Tabasco sauce when seasoning.
5 Crumble the bacon and sprinkle over the chicken when serving.

STUFFED POUSSINS WITH GRAPES

Poussins en Cocotte Véronique

🍽 SERVES 4   🥣 WORK TIME 35-45 MINUTES   ♨ COOKING TIME 1¼ -1½ HOURS

EQUIPMENT

large flameproof casserole with lid

kitchen scissors

medium saucepan

fork

knife

metal spoons

bowls

kitchen paper

kitchen string

platter

slotted spoon

whisk

2-pronged fork

metal skewer

aluminium foil

sieve   baking sheet

In this recipe poussins are stuffed and tied, then roasted en cocotte *in a covered pot. Any small birds such as pigeons or quails can be substituted for poussins. The stuffing is made from a pilaf of couscous, while* véronique *is a classic French garnish of cream and grapes.*

INGREDIENTS

poussins

butter   chicken stock

slivered almonds   arrowroot   couscous

double cream   grapes

vegetable oil   port

metric	SHOPPING LIST	imperial
4	poussins	4
30 g	butter	1 oz
15 ml	vegetable oil, more if needed	1 tbsp
	salt and pepper	
	For the stuffing	
60 g	slivered almonds	2 oz
250 ml	boiling water	8 fl oz
165 g	quick-cooking couscous	5½ oz
30 g	butter	1 oz
	For the sauce	
125 ml	port	4 fl oz
250 g	seedless red or green grapes, removed from stalks	8 oz
250 ml	chicken stock	8 fl oz
10 ml	arrowroot	2 tsp
30 ml	water	2 tbsp
60 ml	double cream	4 tbsp

ORDER OF WORK

1 MAKE THE COUSCOUS STUFFING

2 STUFF AND TIE UP THE POUSSINS

3 COOK THE POUSSINS

4 MAKE THE VERONIQUE SAUCE

1 MAKE THE COUSCOUS STUFFING

1 Heat the oven to 180°C (350°F, Gas 4). Spread the almonds on the baking sheet and toast in the heated oven until browned, 10-12 minutes. Remove the almonds and increase the oven heat to 190°C (375°F, Gas 5).

2 Pour the boiling water over the couscous and allow to stand to absorb the water, about 2 minutes. Alternatively, cook the couscous according to packet instructions.

3 Dice the butter with the knife. Add the diced butter and toasted almonds to the couscous while still hot, then stir with the fork to remove any lumps. Season the stuffing to taste.

2 STUFF AND TIE UP THE POUSSINS

1 Wipe the birds inside and out with kitchen paper. Fill each one with the stuffing, packing it loosely. Pull the flap of skin over stuffing to enclose it.

Pack stuffing lightly because it swells during cooking

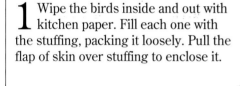

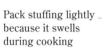

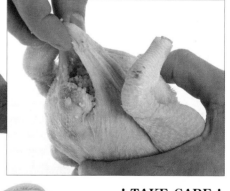

! TAKE CARE !
The birds must be cooked immediately after stuffing because the meat can spoil quickly.

2 Tuck the neck skin and wings under the bird, then pass the string under the tail and tie a knot over the leg joints.

3 Bring the strings along the sides of the body and loop them around the legs. Tie them tightly.

4 Bring the strings under the bird and tie them under the body.

5 Tuck the wing bones behind the back and tie them securely.

3 COOK THE POUSSINS

1 Melt the butter with the oil in the casserole over moderately high heat. Put 2 of the poussins in the pot, breast down, and brown them on all sides, 5-10 minutes. Season with salt and pepper and remove. Repeat the process with the remaining 2 birds, adding more oil if necessary.

2 Replace the birds in the casserole, cover and cook in the heated oven until they are very tender, 50-60 minutes. Test by pricking the thickest part of a thigh with the skewer; the juice should run clear, not pink. Also insert the skewer into the stuffing; it should be hot to the touch when withdrawn. With the slotted spoon, transfer the poussins to the plate. Cover them with foil and keep warm.

Tight-fitting lid prevents poussin juices from evaporating

ANNE SAYS
'The birds will cook more quickly if they are left empty and the stuffing is baked, covered, in a separate dish. Allow 30-40 minutes for the poussins, 10-15 minutes for the stuffing.'

4 MAKE THE VERONIQUE SAUCE

Grapes are flavoured with port

1 In the saucepan, boil the port over high heat until reduced by half. Add the grapes and simmer 1 minute. Lift out the grapes using the slotted spoon and set aside.

2 Discard any fat from the casserole. Add the stock and boil over high heat, stirring to dissolve the pan juices, until reduced by half.

3 Strain the juices into the reduced port. Heat them until boiling, stirring well.

4 Stir the arrowroot and water together to form a smooth paste. Whisk the arrowroot paste into the port mixture. It will thicken at once to form a sauce.

5 Stir the cream into the sauce, then add the grapes and bring back to just boiling. Taste for seasoning.

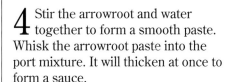

🍴 TO SERVE

Remove the strings from the birds. Set the poussins on individual plates. Spoon some sauce and grapes on the plates. Serve the remaining sauce and grapes separately.

French beans or broccoli are a good accompaniment

Couscous stuffing is scooped out on to plate

V A R I A T I O N

STUFFED POUSSINS WITH CHILLI SAUCE

To complement the couscous stuffing you can make a sauce with Middle Eastern flavourings.

1 Stuff and cook the birds as for Stuffed Poussins with Grapes but serve with the following sauce:

2 Skin, seed and chop 500 g (1 lb) tomatoes. Chop 1 onion and sauté it in 15 ml (1 tbsp) vegetable oil until soft. Add tomatoes, 45 ml (3 tbsp) chicken stock, pinch of ground coriander and 5 ml (1 tsp) harissa (Moroccan chilli sauce) or cayenne to taste. Cook until reduced and thick, 10-20 minutes. Add 60 g (2 oz) chopped stoned black olives. Taste for seasoning.

3 Discard any fat from the pan after cooking the poussins. Dissolve the pan juices in 125 ml (4 fl oz) chicken stock and add to the tomato sauce.

— GETTING AHEAD —

The poussins and sauce can be prepared, up to the end of step 3 of making the sauce, up to 24 hours ahead. Pour the reduced port and stock over the cooked poussins, cover tightly, and keep refrigerated. Before finishing the sauce, reheat the poussins in a 180°C (350°F, Gas 4) oven 20-25 minutes.

CHICKEN MOUSSE WITH MADEIRA BUTTER SAUCE

 SERVES 4 WORK TIME 25-35 MINUTES* COOKING TIME 20-30 MINUTES

EQUIPMENT

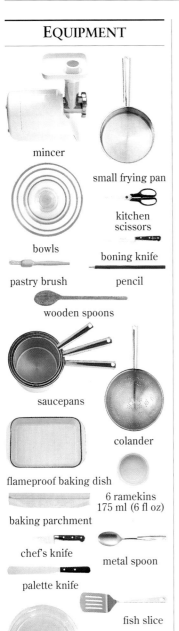

mincer

small frying pan

kitchen scissors

bowls

boning knife

pastry brush

pencil

wooden spoons

saucepans

colander

flameproof baking dish

6 ramekins
175 ml (6 fl oz)

baking parchment

chef's knife

metal spoon

palette knife

fish slice

shallow dishes

whisk   chopping board

metal skewer

This chicken dish – a smooth, creamy mousse wrapped in fine slices of courgette – makes an excellent hot first course, or it can be served as a light main course if saffron rice (see page 87) is added as an accompaniment.

GETTING AHEAD

The chicken mousse can be made 1 day ahead and refrigerated. Reheat in a water bath on top of the stove 10-15 minutes. The sauce should be made shortly before serving. It can be kept warm up to 30 minutes by placing the saucepan in a water bath containing warm water, but it will separate if it gets too hot.

* plus 15-30 minutes chilling time

metric	SHOPPING LIST	imperial
500 g	skinless, boneless chicken breasts	1 lb
2	egg whites	2
	salt and pepper	
	ground nutmeg	
175 ml	double cream	6 fl oz
2	medium courgettes	2
	butter for ramekins	
For the Madeira butter sauce		
2	garlic cloves	2
2	shallots	2
125 g	butter	4 oz
45 ml	Madeira	3 tbsp
15 ml	double cream	1 tbsp

INGREDIENTS

chicken breasts

butter

shallots

garlic cloves

double cream

ground nutmeg

egg whites

Madeira   courgettes

ORDER OF WORK

1 MAKE THE CHICKEN MOUSSE MIXTURE

2 PREPARE THE COURGETTES

3 PREPARE THE RAMEKINS

4 ASSEMBLE AND COOK THE CHICKEN MOUSSE

5 MAKE THE SAUCE AND FINISH THE DISH

1 MAKE THE CHICKEN MOUSSE MIXTURE

1 Remove the tendon from each chicken breast. With the chef's knife, cut the chicken into chunks. Work it through the fine blade of the mincer. Transfer the minced chicken to a medium bowl and set it in a larger bowl of iced water.

ANNE SAYS
'A mincer gives the mousse a light texture. A food processor can be used if you prefer, but take care not to purée too finely.'

Keep mixture cold over iced water while beating in cream

2 Whisk the egg whites until frothy. With a flat wooden spoon, gradually add the egg whites to the chicken, beating the mixture until smooth and firm after each addition. Season with salt, pepper and a pinch of nutmeg. If the mixture is soft, chill to firm it.

ANNE SAYS
'A damp cloth underneath the bowl of iced water holds it steady as you beat.'

3 Beat in the cream, a little at a time. Chill the mixture over the bowl of iced water or in the refrigerator, about 15 minutes or until firm. The mixture should be stiff enough to hold its shape. To test the mixture for seasoning, fry a little piece in the frying pan and taste. Adjust the seasoning if necessary.

2 PREPARE THE COURGETTES

Slice courgettes neatly

1 Trim the courgettes and cut into very thin slices. Bring a saucepan of salted water to the boil. Add courgettes and simmer until softened, 1-2 minutes.

2 Drain the courgette slices in the colander, rinse under cold water to stop the cooking, then drain thoroughly on kitchen paper.

3 PREPARE THE RAMEKINS

Baking parchment keeps mousse from sticking to ramekin

1 Using the base of a ramekin as a guide, draw 6 circles on a sheet of baking parchment. Cut out the paper circles just inside the line.

2 Butter the ramekins. Lay a paper circle in the bottom of each ramekin; brush with butter. Heat oven to 180°C (350°F, Gas 4).

4 ASSEMBLE AND COOK THE CHICKEN MOUSSE

1 Line the bottoms and sides of the ramekins with overlapping slices of courgettes.

Mousse should reach top of courgettes

3 Cover the dish with baking parchment and bake the mousse in the heated oven until the skewer inserted in the centre is hot to the touch when withdrawn, 20-30 minutes. While baking, make the sauce.

! TAKE CARE !
During baking, do not let the water boil or the mousse will separate.

2 Spoon the chicken mousse mixture into the ramekins, smoothing the top. Put the ramekins in the baking dish. Pour in boiling water to come more than halfway up the sides of the ramekins. Bring the water to the boil on top of the stove.

5 MAKE THE SAUCE AND FINISH THE DISH

COLD CHICKEN MOUSSE WITH TOMATO AND MINT COULIS

Chicken mousse is beautiful presented at room temperature with a coulis of fresh tomatoes.

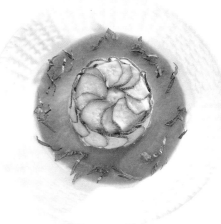

1 Finely chop the garlic. Finely chop the shallots. Heat about 30 g (1 oz) of the butter in a small saucepan, add the garlic and shallots and cook, stirring, 2-3 minutes. Add the Madeira and boil, stirring to dissolve the pan juices, until reduced to a syrupy glaze, 2-3 minutes.

2 Add the cream and boil again until reduced to a glaze. Take the pan from the heat and add the remaining butter, a few pieces at a time, whisking constantly and moving the pan on and off the heat.

! TAKE CARE !
The butter should thicken the sauce creamily without melting to oil. If the sauce gets too hot, it will separate.

Set plate upside-down on ramekin to unmould mousse

🍴 TO SERVE
Using the fish slice and a tea towel, drain excess liquid from the side of each ramekin, then unmould each mousse on to a warm plate and spoon the sauce around.

Hold ramekin in tea towel

1 Prepare and cook mousse as directed in the main recipe. Leave to cool to room temperature.
2 Omit the butter sauce and make a tomato coulis: skin, seed and roughly chop 250 g (8 oz) fresh tomatoes; purée in a food processor until very smooth. With the motor running, gradually add 15 ml (1 tbsp) olive oil to make an emulsion. Season to taste.
3 Unmould the mousse on to individual plates, spoon around the tomato coulis and sprinkle with chopped fresh mint.

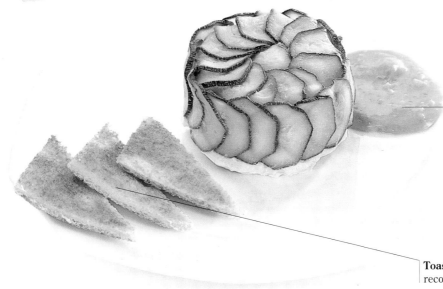

Madeira butter sauce is spooned next to mousse on plate

Toast triangles are recommended accompaniment

CHICKEN POT PIES WITH HERB CRUST

🍽 SERVES 4-6 🥄 WORK TIME 25-35 MINUTES 🍲 COOKING TIME 22-25 MINUTES

EQUIPMENT

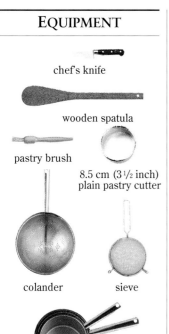

chef's knife

wooden spatula

pastry brush

8.5 cm (3½ inch) plain pastry cutter

colander

sieve

saucepans

whisk

bowls

2 round-bladed knives

large metal spoon

4-6 individual casserole dishes, 11.5 cm (4½ inches) across

chopping board

This is a favourite chicken pot pie recipe of mine with a tasty herb-flavoured scone topping. No accompaniments are needed.

GETTING AHEAD

The filling can be prepared 1 day ahead and refrigerated, but mix the scone dough just before baking the pies.

metric	SHOPPING LIST	imperial
3	medium carrots	3
3	celery sticks	3
1	small bunch of fresh parsley	1
1	medium onion	1
750 g	large potatoes	1½ lb
1 litre	chicken stock	1⅔ pints
175 g	peas	6 oz
1.8 kg	whole cooked chicken	4 lb
	or 500 g (1 lb) cooked skinless, boneless chicken	
60 g	butter	2 oz
30 g	flour	1 oz
175 ml	double cream	6 fl oz
	ground nutmeg	
	salt and pepper	
1	egg	1
For the herb scone topping		
250 g	flour	8 oz
15 ml	baking powder	1 tbsp
5 ml	salt	1 tsp
60 g	butter	2 oz
150 ml	milk, more if needed	¼ pint
1	small bunch of fresh parsley	1

INGREDIENTS

milk

chicken

carrots

potatoes

egg

onion

peas

fresh parsley

celery sticks

chicken stock

double cream

flour

nutmeg

baking powder

butter

ORDER OF WORK

1 MAKE THE FILLING

2 MAKE THE HERB SCONE TOPPING

3 ASSEMBLE AND BAKE THE PIES

1 MAKE THE FILLING

1 Slice the carrots. Trim and thinly slice the celery. Chop the parsley. Chop the onion.

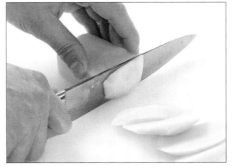

2 Square off the sides of the peeled potatoes. Cut each potato vertically into slices. Stack the slices and cut them into even strips of uniform thickness.

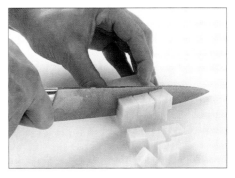

3 Gather the strips together into a pile and slice them evenly crosswise to produce medium dice.

4 Heat the stock to boiling in a large saucepan. Add the carrots, potatoes and celery and simmer 3 minutes.

5 Add the peas and simmer until the vegetables are tender, 5 minutes.

Add well-drained vegetables to slivers of chicken meat

6 Drain the vegetables in the colander, reserving the stock. If using a whole chicken, remove the meat from the bones, discarding all skin and any gristle. Cut the meat into slivers and put in a bowl. Add the vegetables.

7 Melt the butter in a small saucepan over moderate heat. Add the chopped onion and cook until softened but not browned, 3-5 minutes. Sprinkle the flour over the onions and cook, stirring, 1-2 minutes.

Whisk cream into sauce to enrich it

8 Stir in 500 ml (16 fl oz) stock and heat, whisking, until the sauce comes to the boil and thickens. Simmer 2 minutes, then add the cream and a pinch of nutmeg and taste for seasoning.

9 Pour the sauce over the chicken and vegetables, add the chopped parsley and mix gently to combine.

2 MAKE THE HERB SCONE TOPPING

Add just enough milk to bind mixture to dough

1 Sift the flour into a large bowl with the baking powder and salt and make a well in the centre. Add the butter and cut it into small pieces using the round-bladed knives.

2 Rub the mixture with your finger-tips until it forms fine crumbs, lifting and crumbling to aerate it. Chop the parsley and add it to the flour mixture in the bowl.

3 Make a well in the centre, add the milk and cut in quickly with a knife to form coarse crumbs. Add a little more milk if the mixture seems dry.

Knead dough until evenly combined and smooth

4 Mix the dough with your fingers just until it comes together. Turn on to a floured surface and knead lightly for a few seconds until smooth.

! TAKE CARE !
Do not overwork scone dough or it will be tough.

ANNE SAYS
'*If you don't have a pastry cutter, you can use the top of a large glass to cut out rounds.*'

Cut circles close together

5 With your fingers, pat the dough out to 1 cm (½ inch) thickness without stretching it.

6 Cut out rounds with the pastry cutter. Pat out the trimmings and cut additional rounds, for a total of 4-6.

3 ASSEMBLE AND BAKE THE PIES

2 Place a scone round on top of each pie. Beat the egg with pinch of salt and brush the rounds with this glaze. Bake the pot pies in the heated oven 15 minutes. Reduce the heat to 180°C (350°F, Gas 4) and continue baking until the crust is browned and the filling is hot, 7-10 minutes.

1 Heat the oven to 220°C (425°F, Gas 7). Divide the filling evenly among the casserole dishes.

LARGE CHICKEN POT PIE

1 Prepare the filling as directed in the main recipe.
2 Instead of baking the pies in individual dishes, spoon the filling into a medium baking dish.
3 Omit the chopped parsley from the scone dough and cut the rolled dough into 8 rounds, using a 6 cm (2½ inch) pastry cutter.
4 Arrange the rounds over the filling, then glaze and bake them, allowing 15 minutes at 220°C (425°F, Gas 7) and 20-25 minutes at 180°C (350°F, Gas 4).

Filling should be bubbling hot and give off delicious aroma

Scone topping bakes to a rich golden brown

Individual casseroles look attractive but deep ovenproof soup bowls can also be used

GRILLED POUSSINS WITH MUSHROOM SAUCE

Poussins en Crapaudine Dijonnaise

🍽 SERVES 2   🥣 WORK TIME 30-40 MINUTES   🍲 COOKING TIME 35-40 MINUTES

EQUIPMENT

poultry shears

fork

shallow dishes

chef's knife

2-pronged fork

chopping board

saucepans

whisk

kitchen paper

wooden spoon

pastry brush

4 metal skewers

A crapaud *is a toad, which these small birds resemble after they have been flattened on skewers for grilling. Quails are the best substitute for poussins, but a bigger chicken to serve 2 can be used in their place. Pungent Dijon mustard flavours the accompanying mushroom sauce.*

INGREDIENTS

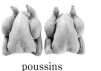
poussins

shallots

mushrooms

watercress

white wine vinegar

dry white wine

butter

chicken stock

Dijon mustard

dried breadcrumbs

garlic clove

flour

metric	SHOPPING LIST	imperial
2	poussins	2
	oil for grill rack	
30 g	butter	1 oz
	salt and pepper	
15 ml	Dijon mustard	1 tbsp
15 g	dried breadcrumbs	½ oz
	bunch of watercress for decoration	
	For the mushroom sauce	
60 g	butter	2 oz
15 g	flour	1 oz
150 g	mushrooms	5 oz
2	shallots	2
1	garlic clove	1
60 ml	medium dry white wine	4 tbsp
60 ml	white wine vinegar	4 tbsp
20 ml	Dijon mustard, or to taste	1½ tbsp
375 ml	chicken stock	12 fl oz

ORDER OF WORK

1 SPLIT AND FLATTEN THE POUSSINS

2 COOK THE POUSSINS

3 MAKE THE MUSHROOM SAUCE

1 SPLIT AND FLATTEN THE POUSSINS

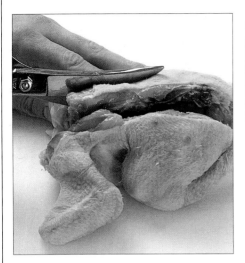

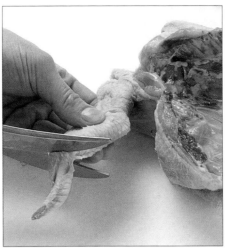

1 Set one bird breast side down on the board. With the poultry shears, cut along each side of the backbone and discard it.

2 Trim any flaps of skin and cut off the wing tips.

3 Force the bird open and snip the wishbone. Wipe the inside of the bird with kitchen paper.

4 Turn the bird breast up with the legs turned in. With the heel of your hand, push down sharply on the breast to break the breastbone and flatten the bird.

Use one hand to exert more pressure on the other

ANNE SAYS
'*Small birds that are split and flattened like this remain moist naturally because the bones disperse the heat. If you are substituting a larger chicken, you will need to baste more frequently with melted butter.*'

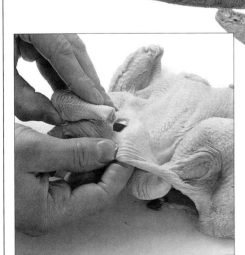

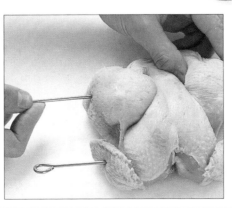

5 Make a small cut in the skin between the leg and breastbone and tuck in the leg knuckles.

6 Thread a skewer through the wings of the bird to hold it flat. Thread a second skewer through the legs. Repeat the procedure for the second bird.

COOK THE POUSSINS

1 Heat the grill. Brush the grill rack with oil. Melt the butter in a small saucepan. Brush the poussins with half of the melted butter and sprinkle them with salt and pepper.

Apply even coating with pastry brush

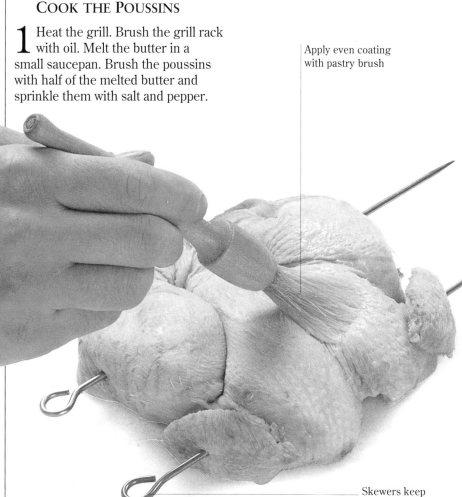

Skewers keep poussin flat during cooking

2 Put the poussins on the grill rack, skin side up. Broil about 7.5 cm (3 inches) from the heat, basting once with butter, about 15 minutes.

3 Turn the birds over with the 2-pronged fork, brush with the remaining butter and grill 10 minutes on the other side.

4 Turn the poussins over again and brush the skin with the mustard, then sprinkle with the breadcrumbs. Grill, skin side towards the heat, until the birds are tender when pierced with the 2-pronged fork, about 10 minutes longer. While the chickens are cooking, make the sauce.

! TAKE CARE !
If the birds brown too quickly at any point during cooking, lower the rack further from the heat.

3 MAKE THE MUSHROOM SAUCE

1 In a shallow dish, mash half of the butter with the flour, using the fork, until soft. Work the mixture to a paste. Set it aside.

ANNE SAYS
'*The paste should be soft so it will combine easily with the sauce liquid. If necessary, work it with your fingers for a moment so the heat of your hand softens the butter.*'

Wipe mushrooms with damp kitchen paper before slicing

2 Clean and slice the mushrooms. Finely chop the shallots. Finely chop the garlic.

3 Melt half of the remaining butter in a medium saucepan. Add the mushrooms and cook, stirring occasionally, until tender and lightly browned, 3-5 minutes.

4 Melt the remaining butter in another saucepan, add the shallots and garlic and cook until softened. Add the wine and vinegar and simmer until reduced to about 30 ml (2 tbsp).

Add browned mushrooms to mustard sauce and cook a few more minutes

5 Add the mustard and stock and stir to combine.

6 Stir in the cooked mushrooms and simmer 5 minutes.

7 Whisk the flour paste into the simmering sauce, a small piece at a time, until the sauce lightly coats the back of a spoon. Season with salt and pepper to taste.

Add butter and flour paste in small pieces, whisking in just enough to thicken sauce to desired consistency

🍽 **TO SERVE**
Twist the stalks off the watercress. Remove the skewers from the poussins. Arrange the birds on plates and decorate with watercress. Spoon on a little sauce, serve the rest separately.

Watercress 'bouquet' adds decorative touch

French fries, the more finely cut the better, are a favourite accompaniment for grilled poussin. The greatest treat is straw potatoes - potatoes cut into julienne and deep fried

GETTING AHEAD
The sauce can be made up to 3 days ahead and kept, covered, in the refrigerator. The poussins can be prepared early in the day for the evening, but grill them just before serving.

V A R I A T I O N

GRILLED CHICKEN WITH GARLIC HERB BUTTER

A larger bird can also be flattened and grilled on skewers as in the Grilled Poussins with Mushroom Sauce. The addition of garlic herb butter under the skin helps keep the bird moist, so you may omit the sauce altogether. Serve garnished with fresh chervil or tarragon. For serving, joint the bird into 4 pieces using a chef's knife and poultry shears.

Herb butter under skin gives attractive appearance to grilled chicken

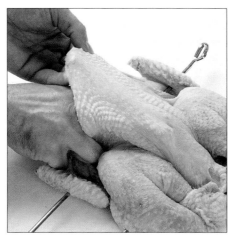

1 Split and flatten a 1.5 kg (3 lb) chicken as directed for the small birds in the main recipe, and insert 2 large skewers to keep it flat.

2 Chop a small bunch each of fresh tarragon and chervil. Finely chop 2 garlic cloves. Using a fork, beat the chopped herbs and garlic into 125 g (4 oz) softened butter. Season to taste with salt, pepper and a squeeze of lemon juice.

3 With your fingers, loosen the skin on the chicken breast. Using a small knife, loosen the skin from the top end of the thigh meat, then ease the skin away from the meat with your fingers.

4 Spread about half of the garlic herb butter between the meat and skin of the legs, using your fingers. Spread the rest of the butter on the meat underneath the breast skin.

5 Cook the chicken as directed, omitting the mustard and dried breadcrumbs. Allow 20 minutes cooking skin side up, 15 minutes skin side down, and a final 10-15 minutes, basting with the pan juices.

COLD CHICKEN AND HAM PIE

 SERVES 8-10 WORK TIME 50-60 MINUTES* 🍲 COOKING TIME 1½ HOURS

EQUIPMENT

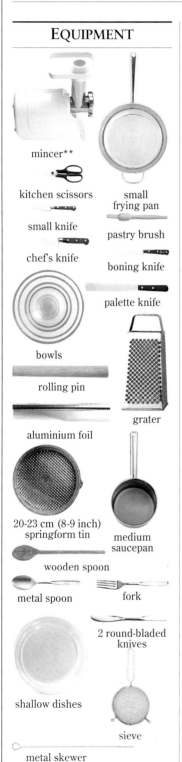

mincer**

kitchen scissors

small frying pan

small knife

pastry brush

chef's knife

boning knife

palette knife

bowls

rolling pin

grater

aluminium foil

20-23 cm (8-9 inch) springform tin

medium saucepan

wooden spoon

metal spoon

fork

2 round-bladed knives

shallow dishes

sieve

metal skewer

** food processor can also be used

A pie that I remember well from my childhood. The tasty butter-and-lard crust encases a filling of chicken and pork, hard-boiled eggs and ham. Wedges of pie are good served with a mixed green salad and with chutney or pickled onions.

GETTING AHEAD

The pie can be made up to 3 days ahead and kept refrigerated, or it can be frozen up to 1 month.

plus 6-8 hours cooling time

metric	SHOPPING LIST	imperial
4	skinless, boneless chicken breasts, total weight about 750 g (1½ lb)	4
375 g	lean boneless pork	12 oz
1	lemon	1
9	eggs	9
5 ml	dried thyme	1 tsp
5 ml	dried sage	1 tsp
	ground nutmeg	
	salt and pepper	
375 g	cooked lean ham	12 oz
	butter for pan	
	For the pastry	
500 g	flour	1 lb
10 ml	salt	2 tsp
75 g	butter	2½ oz
75 g	lard	2½ oz
150 ml	water, more if needed	¼ pint

INGREDIENTS

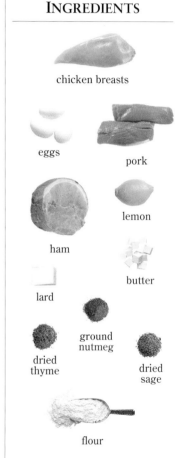

chicken breasts

eggs

pork

lemon

ham

butter

lard

ground nutmeg

dried thyme

dried sage

flour

ORDER OF WORK

1 MAKE THE PASTRY

2 MAKE THE FILLING

3 LINE THE TIN

4 ASSEMBLE AND BAKE THE PIE

1 MAKE THE PASTRY

1 Sift the flour and salt into a large bowl, using the sieve. Make a well in the centre of the flour.

2 Put the butter and lard in the well and cut them into small pieces using the round-bladed knives.

ANNE SAYS
'If you have warm hands, which can make the butter soft when rubbing it in, and result in an oily pastry, you may prefer to make the pastry in a food processor.'

3 Rub the mixture with your fingertips until it forms fine crumbs, lifting and crumbling to aerate it.

Lift your fingers as you rub mixture to incorporate air

4 Make a well in the centre, add the water and mix quickly with a knife to form crumbs. If the mixture seems dry, add 15-30 ml (1-2 tbsp) more water.

5 Mix the dough together with your fingers; it should be soft but not sticky.

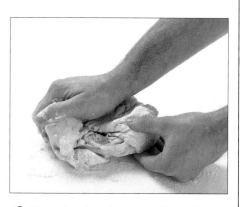

6 Turn the dough on to a floured surface and knead lightly with the heel of the hand until smooth, 5-10 seconds. Wrap the dough and chill 30 minutes in the refrigerator. Meanwhile, make the filling.

2 MAKE THE FILLING

1 Remove the tendon from each chicken breast. Cut 2 of the chicken breasts and the pork into chunks; reserve the remaining 2 chicken breasts.

2 Work the pork and chicken chunks through the fine blade of the mincer, or work them in a food processor. Put the minced meats in a large bowl.

ANNE SAYS
'*A mincer will give a light texture to the filling. If using a food processor, take care not to work too finely.*'

3 Grate the zest from about half of the lemon on to the minced meats in the bowl.

ANNE SAYS
'*To remove all the grated lemon zest from the grater, brush it with a stiff brush.*'

4 With the fork, beat 2 eggs until mixed; add to the minced meats with the thyme, sage, nutmeg, salt and pepper. Mix well with the wooden spoon, then beat the filling until it pulls from the side of the bowl, 3-5 minutes.

Add beaten eggs to meat mixture to help bind it

5 To test the mixture for seasoning, fry a little piece in the small frying pan, turning once, and taste. It should be well seasoned, so add more salt and pepper if required.

Cut chicken and ham into neat cubes for best appearance

6 Cut the reserved chicken breasts and the ham into 2 cm (¾ inch) cubes. Stir the chicken and ham cubes into the filling mixture.

ANNE SAYS
'*To give the finished pie a pretty striped look, the chicken and ham cubes can be spread between the layers of minced filling instead of being mixed in. If you prefer to do this, reserve the chicken and ham cubes until step 2 of Assemble and Bake the Pie – see page 116.*'

3 LINE THE TIN

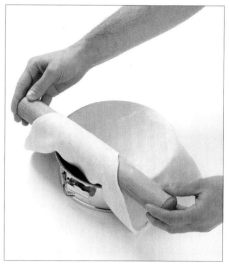

1 Butter the bottom and side of the springform tin.

ANNE SAYS
'You can brush the tin with melted or well-softened butter.'

2 Cut off about three-quarters of the dough and shape it into a ball; keep the remaining dough covered. On a floured surface, roll out the ball of dough into a 5 mm (¼ inch) thick circle that is large enough to line the tin with dough left to overhang. (Test by putting the tin on the dough.)

3 Loosely roll the dough around the rolling pin and unroll it over the prepared tin.

! TAKE CARE !
Do not stretch the dough or it will shrink back during baking.

4 Ease the dough into the tin, pressing it well into the bottom and then against the side. Try to avoid pleats in the side of the dough.

Handle rolled-out dough gently so it does not stretch or tear

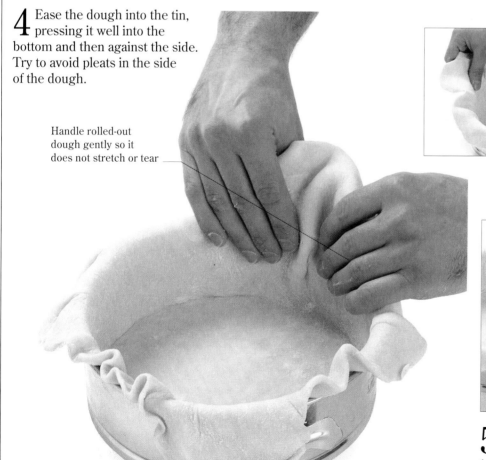

5 Trim the edges of the dough with scissors, leaving about 1 cm (½ inch) overhanging. Add the trimmings to the remaining dough.

4 ASSEMBLE AND BAKE THE PIE

1 Put 6 eggs in a saucepan of cold water, bring to the boil and simmer 10 minutes. Run cold water into the pan to stop the cooking, then allow the eggs to cool. Drain the eggs; tap them on the work surface to crack the shells all over, then peel.

2 Spread half of the filling in the pastry case. Arrange the hard-boiled eggs on top, gently pushing them into the filling. Cover with the remaining filling, ensuring all the gaps are filled.

3 Fold the trimmed dough overhang over the filling. Beat the remaining egg with pinch of salt for the glaze. Brush the edge of the dough with egg glaze.

4 Roll out the remaining dough to a circle about 5 mm (¼ inch) thick. Set the tin on top and cut around the base to form a lid of dough the diameter of the tin.

Use base of tin as guide to cut out lid of dough; reserve trimmings to make decorations for top

5 Lay the lid over the filling and press the edges of dough together to seal.

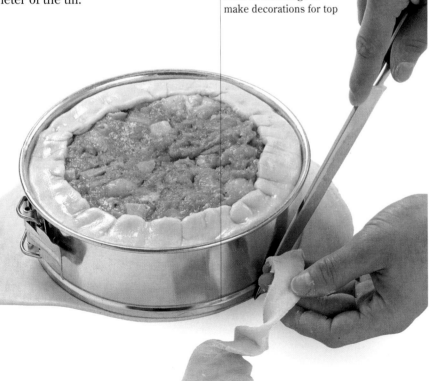

6 Using the skewer, poke a hole in the lid and insert a roll of foil to form a chimney so that the steam can escape during baking.

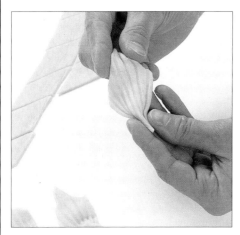

7 Roll out the dough trimmings to 5 mm (¼ inch) thick and cut into strips about 2.5 cm (1 inch) wide. Cut diagonally across the strips to make the leaves. Mark veins on the leaves with the back of the small knife. Curve the leaves with your fingers.

Apply decoration to lid and brush on more glaze

8 Brush the lid with egg glaze. Arrange the leaves on the lid and brush with egg glaze. Chill the pie until firm, about 30 minutes. Meanwhile, heat the oven to 200°C (400°F, Gas 6).

9 Bake the pie until golden brown, about 1 hour. Reduce the heat to 180°C (350°F, Gas 4) and continue baking about 30 minutes longer, until the crust is very brown and the skewer inserted in the stuffing is hot to the touch when withdrawn after 30 seconds. Allow pie to cool, then discard the foil chimney and chill the pie 3-4 hours.

! TAKE CARE !
If the pie is browning too quickly, cover it loosely with foil. If the glaze cracks, brush again with egg just before you lower the oven temperature.

¶◉¶ TO SERVE
Unmould the pie and let it come to room temperature. Serve it whole or cut into generous wedges.

V A R I A T I O N

HOT CHICKEN AND HAM PIE

In France, the hard-boiled eggs would be omitted from this pie and it would be served hot as a first course, with this horseradish cream sauce as an accompaniment.

Whip 250 ml (8 fl oz) double cream until stiff and stir in 30-45 ml (2-3 tbsp) grated fresh horseradish or 45-60 ml (3-4 tbsp) bottled horseradish. Season the sauce to taste.

Chicken and ham chunks surround hard-boiled egg in a herby minced filling

SAUTE OF CHICKEN WITH GARLIC AND WINE VINEGAR

Sauté de Poulet au Vinaigre de Vieux Vin

🍴 SERVES 4 🥣 WORK TIME 15-20 MINUTES 🍲 COOKING TIME 1-1¼ HOURS

EQUIPMENT

kitchen string

large sauté pan
with lid

saucepan

chef's knife

2-pronged fork

wooden spoon

small ladle

whisk

chopping board

conical sieve

ANNE SAYS
'*Herb and other flavoured vinegars can be used in this recipe, each adding its own distinctive taste. When the flavour is concentrated, for example with sherry or balsamic vinegar, you will need only half the amount called for in the recipe.*'

Another variation on the sauté theme, this one has a piquant sauce made with red wine vinegar and chopped tomatoes. The amount of garlic might seem excessive, but its flavour mellows as it cooks, and it acts as a thickening agent for the sauce.

GETTING AHEAD
The chicken can be sautéed and refrigerated in the sauce, covered, up to 2 days.

metric	SHOPPING LIST	imperial
1.5 kg	chicken	3-3 ½ lb
	salt and pepper	
15 ml	vegetable oil	1 tbsp
90 g	butter	3 oz
15	garlic cloves	15
250 ml	red wine vinegar	8 fl oz
15 ml	tomato purée	1 tbsp
2	tomatoes	2
1	bouquet garni	1
250 ml	chicken stock	8 fl oz

INGREDIENTS

chicken

garlic cloves   tomatoes

tomato purée

butter   chicken stock

bouquet garni

vegetable oil   red wine vinegar

ORDER OF WORK

1 PREPARE AND SAUTE THE CHICKEN

2 MAKE THE GARLIC AND VINEGAR SAUCE

1 PREPARE AND SAUTE THE CHICKEN

1 Joint the chicken into 6 pieces (see steps 1-4, How to Joint a Chicken into 8 Pieces, page 29). Alternatively, buy 6 chicken joints. Season the joints with salt and pepper. Heat the oil and 15 g (½ oz) of the butter in the sauté pan over moderate heat until foaming. Add the chicken legs, skin side down, and sauté until they begin to brown, about 5 minutes.

2 Add the chicken breasts and continue cooking gently until very brown, about 10-15 minutes. Turn and brown the other side.

3 Add the unpeeled garlic cloves. Shake the pan gently to distribute the garlic in among the chicken joints, then cover and cook over low heat 20 minutes.

Skins of garlic cloves will be sieved out before serving

119

4 Stir in the vinegar and simmer, uncovered, until reduced by half, about 10 minutes.

Vinegar's acidity is moderated by boiling

5 Add the tomato purée to the pan and stir to mix with the juices in the pan.

ANNE SAYS
'Mix tomato purée in thoroughly and cook briefly to eliminate any raw taste.'

6 Coarsely chop the tomatoes. Add the bouquet garni and tomatoes to the pan and mix into the chicken.

Remove chicken joints as they are cooked and keep warm

7 Cover again and simmer until the chicken joints are tender when pierced with the 2-pronged fork and the juices run clear, 5-10 minutes longer. If some joints are done before others, remove them and keep them warm.

MAKE THE GARLIC AND VINEGAR SAUCE

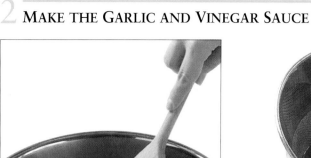

Use small ladle to press garlic pulp through sieve with sauce

1 Remove all the chicken joints from the pan and keep warm. Add the chicken stock to the juices in the pan and boil until well reduced and concentrated in flavour, 3-5 minutes, stirring occasionally.

2 Strain the sauce into the saucepan, pressing hard on the garlic to extract the pulp.

Sautéed potatoes are the traditional accompaniment in Burgundy, where this dish originated

3 Cut the remaining butter into small pieces. Bring the sauce back to the boil, then remove from the heat and add the butter, a few pieces at a time, whisking constantly and moving the pan on and off the heat. Do not boil; the butter should make the sauce creamy without melting to oil. Taste for seasoning.

🍴 TO SERVE

Arrange the chicken joints on individual plates and spoon over the sauce.

French beans are a good complement to the garlic flavour of the sauce

CHICKEN KNOW-HOW

Chicken lends itself to many different recipes and it is sold in many forms and sizes. Choosing the right bird is important, as is knowing how to store it, whether in the refrigerator or freezer. When it comes to thawing a frozen chicken, care is essential, and the meat must also be carefully handled during preparation.

CHOOSING

You will now find a wide variety of chickens in supermarkets, and the following rules hold:

• Fresh chicken is preferable to frozen, but a bird that has been frozen quickly, and then correctly handled, should maintain its quality.

• Skin should be light coloured and moist; if wet, the chicken probably has been poorly frozen.

• A golden colour is not a guide to quality. Yellow skin does not always indicate a cornfed bird but simply the use of yellow foodstuffs.

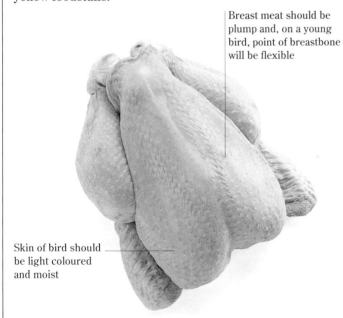

Breast meat should be plump and, on a young bird, point of breastbone will be flexible

Skin of bird should be light coloured and moist

Some butchers and supermarkets carry free-range chickens. Such birds have been fed a good diet (preferably grain), have been allowed to roam in the open air, and can be identified by a generous layer of fat under the skin. They are more expensive than ordinary supermarket birds, but many cooks find their superior flavour and texture make them worth the price.

The label will also give the weight, which is useful when considering cooking methods. Young tender birds are good for grilling, barbecuing, frying and roasting. Traditionally, the larger the bird, the better the flavour. Fat develops under the skin and in the meat, making it more tender when cooked. However, when buying a large chicken of 2.25 kg (5 lb) or more, be sure it is not too old to roast. Such an old hen is aptly called a boiling fowl because its meat is tough. Poaching or braising will make it tender, while the cooking liquid forms the basis for a rich, full-flavoured sauce.

Almost all chickens are sold cleaned with their innards removed. The giblets (neck, gizzard, heart and liver) are in the cavity, so be sure to remove them. Neck, gizzard, and heart are good for stock (see page 124); the liver can be chopped to flavour a sauce, gravy or a stuffing.

STORING FRESH CHICKEN

A cleaned, fresh chicken can be kept in the refrigerator for up to two days. Discard any tight plastic wrapping and cover the bird loosely. If wrapped in butcher shop paper, unwrap it, place on a large dish and cover loosely.

FREEZING

When freezing a whole bird, remove and wrap any giblets separately. If you truss a whole chicken with string before freezing, it will be ready for cooking when thawed. Put the bird in a plastic freezer bag and overwrap it with aluminium foil. Chicken pieces can also be frozen, wrapped first in a layer of plastic, then foil.

Cooked chicken can be frozen with or without bones, but tends to dry out if kept for longer than two weeks. However, when covered with sauce or poaching liquid, it freezes well for up to three months if tightly wrapped.

! TAKE CARE !
Never refreeze raw chicken and do not freeze stuffed birds because the stuffing will not freeze sufficiently to prevent bacteria from developing.

THAWING

It is best to let a chicken thaw in the refrigerator; allow approximately three hours per 500 g (1 lb). To speed thawing time, place the bird in its original plastic wrapping in the sink or a large bowl and cover with cold water. Change the water regularly until the chicken thaws. Using this method, a large bird will thaw in three to five hours.

! TAKE CARE !
A frozen bird should be cooked within 12 hours of thawing.

CLEANING AND HANDLING

Do not rinse a chicken before cooking; just wipe out the cavity with damp kitchen paper. If the chicken has been frozen, blot the skin with dry kitchen paper to absorb as much moisture as possible.

Always wash your hands thoroughly before and after handling raw chicken. Chopping boards, knives, food processors and other items of kitchen equipment, should be scalded with hot water and thoroughly washed before being used in the preparation of other ingredients. These are preventive measures to destroy possible salmonella bacteria that could contaminate other foods.

STORING COOKED CHICKEN

Chicken should stand no more than an hour at room temperature after cooking. If keeping longer than this, store it loosely wrapped in the refrigerator and use within three days. If the chicken has a strong sauce or stuffing, it should be eaten within 24 hours. Stuffing and gravy can be stored separately in covered containers and reheated just before serving. Be sure the gravy reaches boiling point.

SIZES AND SERVINGS

Chickens are available in many sizes. The servings given are approximate, depending on your appetite and the amount of other ingredients in the recipe.

• Poussins and small cock birds (coquelets) normally weigh about 500 g (1 lb) and serve one person. Other white-fleshed birds, which can be directly substituted for poussins, include quail, bred to serve one or two people.

• Frying or grilling chickens of under 1.5 kg (3 lb) serve two to four people. They can be bought whole or cut in half or pieces.

• Whole roasting chickens weighing over 1.5 kg (3 lb) are more mature, fatter birds. Chickens of this size should serve at least four people.

SALMONELLA BACTERIA

! TAKE CARE !

Poultry is particularly susceptible to contamination by salmonella bacteria, which causes food poisoning. It is vitally important that chicken be handled and prepared carefully:

• If storing raw chicken, keep it loosely wrapped in the refrigerator for no more than two days.
• Thaw frozen birds completely before cooking.
• Bring all birds to room temperature before cooking.
• Wash your hands and all equipment before and after handling the raw flesh.
• Stuff the cavity loosely, or do not stuff it at all so that heat penetration kills any salmonella bacteria.
• Cook chicken thoroughly for best flavour and to protect against salmonella. Pieces should fall easily from a two-pronged fork and the juice running from the thigh should be clear. To check if a chicken is cooked, lift it up and tip it so the juices run from the cavity – they should be clear not pink.
• Because some microwave ovens produce inadequate cooking temperatures, I do not advocate using a microwave oven for cooking or reheating chicken .

• Large chickens are often sold cut up into pieces. Individual parts are also sold in packages.

• Boiling fowl (sometimes called stewing chickens) are mature hens weighing more than 2.25 kg (5 lb) that serve at least six people. Boiling fowl are best with plenty of liquid (braised or poached). A cock, a mature male bird, is found only in country markets and a few speciality shops. The meat is dark, resembling a game bird. A fowl or large roasting chicken is the best alternative.

• Capons are neutered cock birds, very plump and white. They are specially fattened to yield large amounts of breast meat, weigh up to 4.5 kg (10 lb), and serve 10 to 12 people.

Poussin

Coquelet

Boiling Fowl

Chicken

Capon

CHICKEN STOCK

Chicken stock is an indispensable ingredient in many sauces and soups. It keeps well up to 3 days, covered, in the refrigerator, and it also freezes well. Stock is often reduced to concentrate for a recipe, so salt and pepper are not added while it is cooking.

🍴◉ MAKES ABOUT 3½ PINTS

🥣 WORK TIME 15 MINUTES

🍲 COOKING TIME UP TO 3 HOURS

SHOPPING LIST

1 kg	raw chicken backs and necks, or 1 whole stewing chicken	2-2½ lb
1	onion	1
1	carrot	1
1	celery stick	1
1	bouquet garni	1
5	peppercorns	5
2 litres	water, more if needed	3½ pts

1 Put the chicken in a large saucepan. Quarter the onion, carrot and celery stick and add to the pan with the bouquet garni and peppercorns.

2 Add water just to cover the ingredients. Bring to the boil and simmer up to 3 hours, skimming occasionally. If using a stewing chicken, remove it when the thigh is tender when pierced with a skewer, 1¼-1½ hours. It can then be used in a recipe calling for cooked chicken meat.

ANNE SAYS
'The longer the stock simmers, the more flavour it has.'

3 Strain the stock into a large bowl. Cool, then cover and keep in the refrigerator.

ANNE SAYS
'If you do not make stock at home, buy good canned consommé (preferably low sodium so that you can control seasoning) or use bouillon cubes.'

BASIC TECHNIQUES
REMOVING A WISHBONE

Fold back the neck skin of the chicken. With the point of a knife, loosen the wishbone and remove it. Also remove any fat. When the wishbone is removed, breast meat is easy to carve into thin slices.

JOINTING CHICKEN INTO 8 PIECES

Using a chef's or boning knife, cut down between the leg joint and body on one side. Twist the bone sharply outwards to break the joint, then cut through and pull the leg from the body. Repeat this procedure for the other leg.

Slit chicken closely along the breastbone to loosen the meat, then split the breastbone with a chef's knife or poultry shears. Turn the bird over and cut the rib bones and backbone from the breast in one piece, leaving the wing joints attached to the breast. The two halves of the bird are now divided into four pieces of meat.

Cut each breast piece in half diagonally, so that some meat is included with the wing bone. Cut off any sharp bones. This makes 6 pieces.

Cut each leg in half through the joint, between the thigh and the drumstick, using the line of fat as a guide. Now there are 8 pieces.

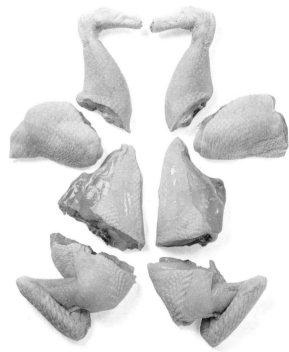

REMOVING A TENDON

Strip the tendon from the centre of the breast by stroking with a boning knife. If the inner fillet becomes detached, replace it. Pull off any skin and discard.

TRUSSING

Wipe the inside of the chicken with kitchen paper and season with salt and pepper. Remove the wishbone. Set the bird breast up and push the legs back and down. Insert a threaded trussing needle at the knee joint, push through the bird and out through the other knee joint. Turn the bird back-side up. Pull the neck skin over the neck cavity and tuck the wing tips over it. Push the needle through both sections of one wing into the neck skin, and continue under the backbone to the other side. Push the needle through both wing bones of the second wing. Turn the bird on its side. Pull the ends of the string firmly together and tie securely. Turn the bird breast up. Tuck the tail into the cavity of the bird and fold over the top skin. Push the needle through the skin. Loop the string round one drumstick, under the breastbone and over the other drumstick. Tie the ends of the string together.

CARVING

Remove the trussing string. With a carving or chef's knife, cut down between the leg and the body. Turn the bird on its side and cut round the oyster meat so it remains attached to the thigh. Turn the bird on its back. Twist the leg sharply outwards to break the joint, then cut through the joint and pull the leg from the body. Repeat the procedure for the other leg. Halve the leg by cutting through the joint, using the line of white fat as a guide. Cut horizontally above the wing joint, through to the breastbone, so you can carve a complete slice of breast meat. Carve the breast in slices parallel to the rib cage. Cut off the wing. Carve the other side in the same way.

BONING COOKED CHICKEN

Using a boning knife, cut down between the leg and body joints. Twist the leg sharply outwards to break the joint, then cut through the joint and pull the leg from the body. Repeat for the other leg. Slit along one side of the chicken breast-bone. Using your fingers and the point of the knife, loosen the breast meat from the carcass, removing the breast half in one piece. Repeat for the other breast. Pull away the wishbone and the meat adhering to it. Pull off any remaining meat from the carcass. Pull off the skin from the pieces and discard. Shred the meat with your fingers and pile on a plate. Using your fingers and the point of the knife, tear and cut the meat from the leg bones. Trim away the tendons, discard the skin and shred the meat.

HOW-TO BOXES

*There are pictures of all preparation steps for each **Chicken Classics** recipe. Some basic techniques are used in a number of recipes; they are shown in extra detail in these special 'how-to' boxes:*

INDEX

ACKNOWLEDGEMENTS

Photographer David Murray
Photographer's Assistant Jules Selmes

Chef Eric Treuille
Cookery Consultant Linda Collister
Home Economist Annie Nichols

UK Editor José Northey
Indexer Sally Poole

Typesetting Rowena Feeny
Debbie Rhodes
Text film by Disc To Print (UK) Limited

Production Consultant Lorraine Baird

*Carroll & Brown Limited
would like to thank Colin Walton and
Sarah Summerbell for design input.
ICTC (081-568-4179) supplied the Cuisinox Elysee
pans used throughout the book and The Kitchenware
Merchants Limited provided the Le Creuset cookware.
Moulinex/Swan Holdings Limited supplied
the deep-fat fryer and mincer.*

*Anne Willan
would like to thank her chief editor
Cynthia Nims and associate editor Kate Krader
for their vital help with writing the book and
researching and testing the recipes, aided by
La Varenne's chefs and trainees.*